THE SKEAN

THE DISTINCTIVE FIGHTING KNIFE OF GAELIC IRELAND,

1500-1700

ROBERT GRESH

SCHIFFER MILITARY
4880 Lower Valley Road   Atglen, PA 19310

OTHER SCHIFFER BOOKS ON RELATED SUBJECTS

Combat Knives and Knife Combat: Knife Models, Carrying Systems, Combat Techniques,
Dietmar Pohl and Jim Wagner, 978-0-7643-4834-1

Fairbairn-Sykes Fighting Knife: Collecting Britain's Most Iconic Dagger,
Wolfgang Peter-Michel, 978-0-7643-3763-5

The Puukko: Finnish Knives from Antiquity to Today,
Anssi Ruusuvuori, 978-0-7643-6070-1

Designed by Christopher Bower
Cover design by Christopher Bower
Type set in Carta Marina/Adobe Caslon Pro

ISBN: 978-0-7643-6637-6
Printed in China

Published by Schiffer Publishing, Ltd.
4880 Lower Valley Road
Atglen, PA 19310
Phone: (610) 593-1777; Fax: (610) 593-2002
Email: Info@schifferbooks.com
Web: www.schifferbooks.com

For our complete selection of fine books on this and related subjects, please visit our website at www.schifferbooks.com. You may also write for a free catalog.

Schiffer Publishing's titles are available at special discounts for bulk purchases for sales promotions or premiums. Special editions, including personalized covers, corporate imprints, and excerpts, can be created in large quantities for special needs. For more information, contact the publisher.

We are always looking for people to write books on new and related subjects. If you have an idea for a book, please contact us at proposals@schifferbooks.com.

DEDICATION

To the hospitable people of Williamstown, County Galway, who work to preserve the heritage of Templetogher, by my grandfather's native place, and whose forbearers were said to have been troubled on occasion by *Nuala na Miodóg*, a formidable *scian*-wielding fairy.

ACKNOWLEDGMENTS

This study makes frequent reference to the pioneering work of the late Etienne Rynne, gathering it under one cover and expanding upon it. Thanks to Margaret Lannin of NMI, and Matthew Potter of the Limerick Museum and Paul Rondelez. All conclusions and any mistakes are entirely my own.

CONTENTS

PREFACE

It must be noted at the outset that the surviving corpus of known Irish skeans that forms the basis of this study is relatively quite small. In fact, the type was not recognized until the 1980s, and it is to be hoped that time will add to the number of available examples. The humble goal of this publication is to raise awareness of this uniquely Irish weapon.

This work is chiefly indebted to the late Etienne Rynne, who first recognized the surviving skeans for what they were. Professor Rynne published his findings in his beloved *North Munster Antiquarian Journal* and other periodicals that have been relatively difficult to access.

The call for a new focus on Gaelic Ireland in the Late Medieval / Early Modern periods received great impetus in 2001 with the publication of *Gaelic Ireland, ca. 1250–ca. 1650.* In that landmark collection of essays on the long-neglected subject of Gaelic Ireland, the editors cited the work of Etienne Rynne in identifying the skean as a "distinctively Irish weapon," and noted that it was "this sort of close scholarly attention over a whole range of artifacts and site types that will in time contribute to the overall understanding of cultural diversity and contiguity in Ireland after ca. 1250."[1]

In the words of professor G. A. Hayes-McCoy, whose own work focused on identifying and describing the distinctive Irish sword types from our period of study: "Thus is added one more piece of evidence to what we know of the distinctive character of native Irish society before the Tudor conquest steamrolled institutions, costumes, weapons and everything else into the flat pattern of an interpreted internationalism."[2]

INTRODUCTION

Against the light foote Irish have I serued, and in my skinne bare tokens of their skenes.
—*Solimon and Persida*, 1599

The distinctive fighting knife used by the Gaelic Irish in the Late Medieval / Early Modern period is the skean (Ir. *scian*, pronounced "shkeen"), rendered variously in English as "skean," "skayne," etc. It was an acutely pointed, single-edged knife very similar to the more well-known Scottish dirk.

The skean could be short enough to be hidden about the body and flung like a missile, end over end. This shorter skean is sometimes called *miodóg*. Much-longer versions had blades up to 22" in length and can be referred to as *scian fada*, rendered variously in English as "long knives" or "long skeans." All are without a guard, and two styles of handle carving can be distinguished.

The ultimate origin of the skean may lie in the seax used by the Hiberno-Norse in the Viking era, but archeological and literary evidence for the skean extends back only to the Late Medieval period. Its exact relationship to the Highland Scottish dirk is unclear, since while the blades resemble one another, the handles and sheaths are quite distinct. And whereas the earliest form of Highland dirk is not attested before ca. 1600, the Irish skean is identified as a distinctive knife in the historical record during the Tudor era.

Four examples each of the shorter and seven of the longer skean have survived (see fig. 1, *below*), and all are described in part B after a review of the documentary evidence.

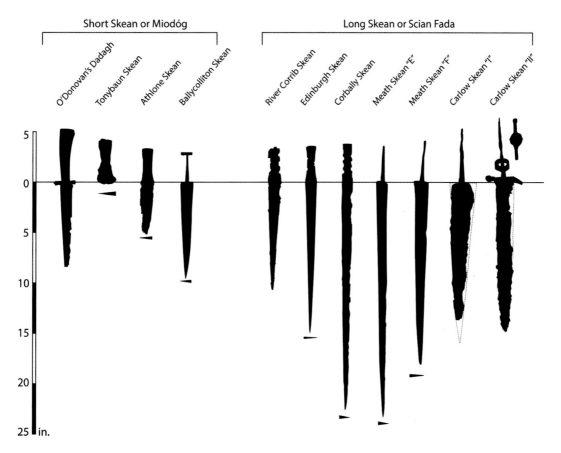

Fig. 1. Skean family

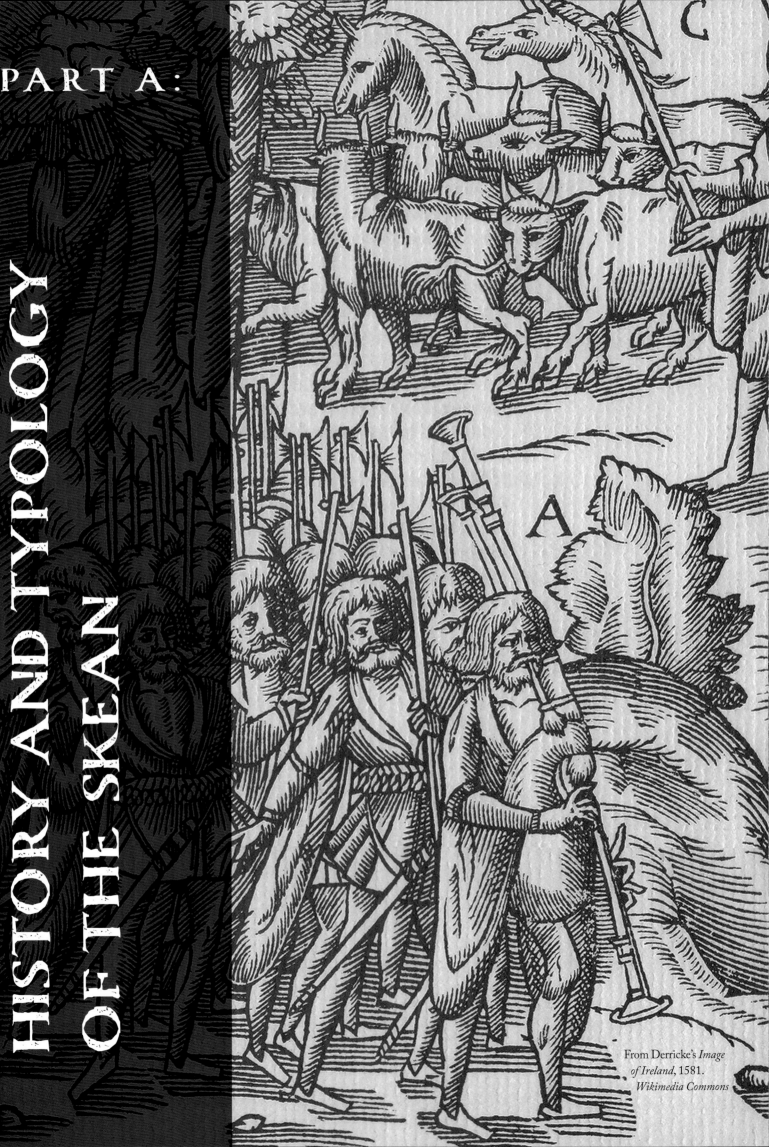

PART A:

HISTORY AND TYPOLOGY
OF THE SKEAN

From Derricke's *Image
of Ireland*, 1581.
Wikimedia Commons

CHAPTER 1

HISTORY OF THE SKEAN

ORIGINS

Weather these skeyns were the sort of knives called Seaxes, by the ancient Saxons, must be left to the inquiry of others.
   —Smith, *History of Cork*, 1749

The suggestion that the Irish skean may derive from the seax family of Germanic Migration-era knives was first made in 1749 (*above*) and remains plausible.[1]

The surviving skeans we will examine in part B were found without datable context but seem unlikely to be earlier than the sixteenth or seventeenth centuries. The seax theory is challenged by the fact that the skean does not appear in Viking-era finds, nor is there any traceable development leading up to the Late Medieval period.

There are two kinds of Germanic seax that might be seen as forerunners of the long and short skean of late medieval Ireland: the narrow longseax and narrow seax. But these were out of use by ca. 600 CE, and seax blades lack the acutely tapered thrusting point found in all skean blades.

It is in the surviving skean sheaths that we see some of the best evidence of a possible seax connection. The Kilcumber and Edinburgh skean sheaths are closely matched by some Viking-era seax sheaths from Dublin and Coppergate, two examples of which are shown opposite. These have a cuplike upper section that envelops the handle, as found on the later Irish skean sheaths. Note the interlaced saltier or St. Andrew's cross pattern on the upper section of the sheath on the left, which appears in the same location on the skean sheaths. The sheath on the right has a stepped or "key" pattern running along its seam edge, which also appears on the Kilcumber sheath, and the panel of interlace filling the lower section is also repeated on the skean sheaths.

Fig. 2. Seax sheaths tooled with motifs similar to those found on the sixteenth/seventeenth-century Irish sheaths

In terms of decoration, there is a surviving "princely" Frankish seax with a bronze handle whose horizontal and diagonal bands of interlace seem to presage the motifs later seen on Irish skeans (fig. 3, *left*). But it is dated to ca. 600 CE, and again the form of the handle and blade does not coincide with the late medieval / early modern skeans.

Rather, the "Celtic" interlace on Irish skeans and their sheaths is generally understood to be a conscious revival of ancient forms, emblematic of the Gaelic political and cultural resurgence in late medieval Ireland. Other examples of this conscious antiquarianism are the tooling on the leather satchel of the *Book of Armagh*, and the carving on the Trinity harp.[2]

The skean blades are in fact most comparable to those found on certain European ballock and rondel daggers of the fourteenth to sixteenth centuries—stiff and wickedly pointed with a single cutting edge. While having an edge, they are primarily thrusting blades, with the ability to pierce mail or seek out the gaps in plate armor. This is the sort of blade most commonly found on rondel daggers, and most of the ballock daggers recovered from the 1545 wreck of the *Mary Rose* have had blades of this description as well.[3]

While the handle shapes of ballock and rondel daggers are different than those of the Irish skean, the rondel handles were sometimes carved with a spiral twist.

The word *scian* itself is thought to be quite old. It is one of a cluster of Irish words related to seax, and all having to do with knives, cutting, or cleaving. They all are constructed using "sc," which derives from Proto-Indo-European *sec*, and seem to reflect splitting and chipping stone, and cutting with the resultant blade. Along with *scian* itself we thus have *sclata* (slate), *scaineadh* (crack, split), *scealla* (shale, chip), *scaineach* (thin, cracked), *scean* (crack split), and *scailp* (chasm or cleft).[4]

Considering the close affinity between the cultures of Gaelic Scotland and Ireland, it seems natural to connect the Irish skean and Scottish dirk. Indeed, it is sometimes asserted that the Scottish Highland dirk and the Irish skean were one and the same. An examination of the evidence for the emergence of the earliest form of Highland dirk will reveal that there is actually significant divergence between the two forms of knife.

Fig. 3, *left* and *right*. Frankish seax handle with interlace decoration in horizontal and diagonal bands. *Far right*: Ballock dagger with handle carved in a barley twist.

SCOTTISH CONNECTIONS

Charles E. Whitelaw's typology for the Highland dirk was set out in 1905 and has not been superseded. His first and earliest type is derived directly from those dudgeon daggers that had a thick-backed, single-edged blade. The dudgeon dagger itself had evolved in Lowland Scotland from the ballock dagger common to Europe from the fourteenth to sixteenth centuries.[5]

Whitelaw places this first type of dirk no earlier than ca. 1600, and it is superseded by the fully developed dirk by ca. 1700. A more conservative author has recently placed its appearance closer to ca. 1650.[6] It is characterized by a broad, flat pommel; a cylindrical handle; and haunches that are deeper and more narrow than those of the dudgeon dagger. The grip is less than 3" long, and the fingers were intended to wrap around the haunches as well. Two horizontal bands of carved interlace usually encircle the handle. This interlace would eventually cover the entire grip after ca. 1700.

All of this contrasts with the handles of Irish skeans, which are elegantly waisted and lack the flared pommel cap and haunches of the dirk. The grips of the Irish skeans are generally fitted with iron ferrules top and bottom and are deeply carved with bands of interlace in either a spiral or Saint Andrew's cross pattern. Notably, the Irish grips are long enough to comfortably accommodate the whole of the hand.

The blades of Whitelaw's first type of dirk are, however, much in keeping with those of the Irish skean. Both had a large triangular-section blade, single edged and thick backed, the straight sides tapering to an acute point with its tip in the centerline. The flat-section tang was also in the centerline. There was no curve suggestive of a carving knife, and the blades were without the fluting or notching often found later. The great difference is that while the first type of dirk is generally about 15" long overall, with a blade from 10" to 12", the skean could often have a blade 22" or longer in length.

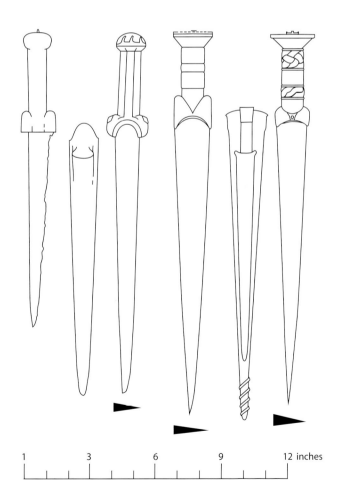

Fig. 4, *left*: Whitelaw's progression from ballock to dudgeon to dirk. The earliest form of dirk is without interlace carving on the bands encircling the grip.

1   3   6   9   12 inches

The word "dirk" itself is of unknown origin, and the proper name in Scots Gaelic is *biodag*. The earliest recorded instance of the word comes from the Inverness Burgh records of 1557, where a "dowrk" is stated to have been wrongfully drawn and broken on a man's head. Later in the century, dirk makers are noted in Edinburgh, the word being spelled variously durck, dorks, and durches. All of these sixteenth-century references to dirks in Scottish contexts are thought to refer to the standard European ballock knife.[7]

An effigy at Ardchattan Priory, dated 1502, is sometimes cited as an early representation of a dirk.[8] However, the dagger represented in the effigy, hanging at the belt of Alan MacDougall, is identified by authorities on late medieval Highland sculpture as a ballock knife by its tapered grip and rounded lobes.[9] The reader may judge for himself from the image below.

Scian (*sgian* in Scots Gaelic) is simply the word for "knife" in modern Irish, but in our period of study, it most frequently refers to a fighting knife in Irish contexts. Interestingly, there is a satirical song in Scots Gaelic, "Tha biodag air Mac Thòmais" ("Thompson's Dirk"), that seems to indicate that a distinction may sometime have been made between a dirk and a *sgian*. The song appears to contrast the wearing of a *biodag*, or richly mounted dirk, with the wearing of a *sgian*, or ordinary knife. Apparently, a *biodag* implied a certain status, so that anyone who carried one without being recognized as entitled to it was subjected to the satirist's barbs:

Tha boidag air Mac Thòmais,
's gur math gu fòghnadh sgian dha.

Thomas's son wears a dirk,
though well would a knife suffice him.[10]

The word *duirc* does appear in later Irish sources, but etymology reveals it to be a direct borrowing of the English word "dirk." James Farewell's doggerel satire, the *Irish Hudibras* (1689), says of certain Irish characters:

. . . with their *Durgins* and *Madoges*
They cut upon their greasie Brogues

As we have seen, madoge *(miodóg)* was an Irish term sometimes used for the shorter variety of skean, and it is cognate with the Scots Gaelic *biodag*. The form "durgin" (*duirceann*) appears in the seventeenth-century Irish bardic satire *Pairlement Chloinne Tomáis*, where it is specifically applied to the dull, rusty cleavers carried by the despised peasantry. The bitter bardic author, having lost his status in the wake of the Tudor reconquest, contrasts these upstart Gaelic rabble with the kerns of old and their "edges of prowess and encounter and of razor-sharp weapons."[11]

The *sgian dubh* or "black knife," worn tucked in the hose top with modern Highland dress, should be mentioned here. It is generally considered a product of the Romantic-era revival of Highland dress initiated by king George IV's visit to Edinburgh in 1822.[12]

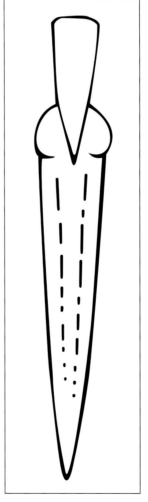 

Fig. 5, *left*: The dagger represented on the effigy of Alan MacDougall at Ardchattan, after Steer and Bannerman. *Right*: The eponymous *sgian* of Skene of that ilk, preserved in the family charter chest. *PD-US-expired*

SKENE OF THAT ILK

According to tradition, a prominent Aberdeenshire family of Gaelic origin, Skene, of Skene, owed their name and arms to an ancestor's heroic action with a skean. While it seems more likely that the family simply took its name from an ancient territorial designation, the apocryphal story is of interest in illustrating the use of the word "skean" as a synonym for dirk in early Scotland.

The story is recorded in a manuscript (MS.A) in the charter chest of Skene that gives the family origin according to Alexander Skene in 1678: "Ane old tradition is that the tribe and family of Skein had their origin from Struan Robertson of Athole, and they from McDonald, and that our first author was a son of the Laird of Struans, and had his first donation immediately from the king, for killing ane devouring wolfe in the forest, near the freedom land of Aberdeen, for which he got ye confirmation of East and Wester Skein, to the freedom of Aberdeen, and that with ane coat of arms . . . relating to the valorous act, viz., 3 wolf's heads crazed upon the points of 3 Skeens, triumphant in a field of Gules."[13]

Two years later, a second manuscript account by George Mackenzie says, "A second son of Struan Robertson, for killing of a wolf in Stocket Forrest by a dirk in the king's presence, got the name of Skein, which signifies dirk in Irish, and three dirk-points in pale for his armes."[14] The

Fig. 6, The arms of Skene of that ilk, from *The Heraldic Plates* of Alexander Nisbet (1657–1725), published in 1893. *Creative Commons 4.0*

supporters are described in a third manuscript (MS.B): "Supported on the dexter by a Dunewassell in highland habit, viz., a blue bonnet, pinched up on the left syde with a bon pin, a slashed out coat or doublet, enveloped with a plaid over his left shoulder, and girded in his sword, and his left hand curving up the shield, and in his right hand a Skene or dagger guarding it, and on the sinister syd a Gillieweetfoot, with his master's target on his left arme, and his doorlach pendant to his heels, with short hoise, and rullions on his foot."[15]

EARLY HISTORICAL NOTICES

The *Book of Magauran* (ca. 1303–1362) makes reference to hafted skeans (*sgian eamhdha*) and a warrior split "down to his knife-belt" (*crios sgeine*).[16] The poem *The Triumphs of Turlough* (1389) contains the rare word *ennach*, which has been translated as dirk: "This same round-star-studded belt, in which was hitched a long blue-gleaming dirk (*ennach*) hanging ready to hand; it was strong in the point, thick-backed, thin-edged, and had a decorated wooden haft."[17] From this description, it is likely what was latter called a skean.

The skean is identified by name as a distinctive Irish weapon in 1418, when the *Calendar of Carew Manuscripts* under that year describes "sixteen hundred Irishmen armed in mail with darts and skaynes" arriving at the Siege of Rouen.[18] The French chronicler Monstrelet, describing the same force, says, "They had a targe, a bundle of small darts, and a great knife carried at the waist."[19] Sir John Froissart's *Chronicle*, discussing these same troops, says, "The Irish have pointed knives; with broad blades, sharp on both sides like a dart-head, with which they kill their enemies."[20] Froissart's description of the knives as double edged is at variance with all other evidence, which indicates the skean was invariably single edged.

TUDOR AND STUART NOTICES

A skean appears among the arms of the kern, who were the Irish light foot of the Tudor era. We read, for example, "Every kern hath . . . 3 speares, a swerd & a skene,"[21] or "The Kernagh . . . his armour is but light and slender, being . . . a target and sword, a skeine, and three or foure dartes."[22] But the skean was not necessarily a lowly object and could be among the valuable gifts exchanged by Irish chiefs to establish alliances and fealty. In 1588 the State Papers accuse Brian O'Rourke of writing in Irish to McMahon, saying, "He has not a good harp in his country but sends two great spears and two skeans."[23] This was a common practice among the Irish chiefs, since a year later the same source records Fergus O'Farrell being accused of treason for having "sent a harp as a token to Feagh M'Hugh" and his son having visited Feagh for a week, receiving at his departure "a dag from Feagh M'Hugh and a chief horse as a bond of his devotion." Indeed, the poet Tadhg Dall Ó hUiginn (1550–1591) addressed a poem to a skean called *Gráinne*, a "precious weapon," with clear hopes of being awarded with the skean as payment! (see appendix).

The skean features in a premature notice of the demise of the hated Feagh M'Hugh O'Byrne in June 1595, which states hopefully, "Feagh himself was shot in the thigh and hurt with a skeyne in the body; for confirmation of this it is affirmed that at the time they got his helmet, target and the sword out of his hand."[24]

SHORT SKEAN, OR *MIODÓG*

Luke Gernon wrote of the kern in 1620: "And for his weapon he weares a skeyne, which is a knife of three fingers broad of the length of a dagger and sharpening towards the poynt, with a rude wooden handle. He weares it poynt blanke at his codpiece."[25] This shorter type of skean appears in the State Papers in 1582, in which "Captain Macworth was attacked by Melaghlen Roe O'Kelly with a short knife termed a meddock and wounded in the arm."[26] The State Papers refer to a hidden skean on November 20, 1589, when the Burkes complain that John

Carie, undersheriff of Mayo, came to Creigh and met Thomas Roe Burke: "Carie . . . said unto Thomas, methink you have a skene"; "I have one," said Thomas, "but it shall do you no harm." "Give it to me," said Carie."[27] Thomas was slain in the subsequent struggle.

This word *miodóg* is used for "dagger" in modern Irish, and historically it recurs as a term for the shorter skean. Walker's *Dress of the Irish* mentions it: "Long, loose, uniformly yellowish (not yellow) gowns and the middogues or dirks were the principal robes of the Irish chieftains."[28] Two soldiers who arrested the rebel Edward Butler of Urlingford, a person of high rank, in 1652 were examined and stated that when they arrested him they found hidden on him "a maddeogue, or skean, with the haft in his hand and the blade in the sheath."[29]

A fragment of nineteenth-century *seanachus*, or folklore, from Donegal refers to the disarming of the MacSweenys, formerly galloglass to O'Donnell, following the conquest of Ulster and the imposition of the British peace. Their traditional weapon, the *tuagh*, or battle ax, was banned. Rather than face life entirely disarmed, "they carried a knife called in Gaelic both in Ireland and Scotland a *meadóg*, whence they have been termed *Clann tSuibhne na Meadóg*. Carried in a leather belt, it was inconspicuous under a *cóta mór*."[30] Thus the *meadóg* could not have been a knife of very large proportions. A land agent finally broke the MacSweenys of this habit of carrying a *meadóg* by accepting a *meadóg* in lieu of half a year's rent, "so that you might offer to-day a huge reward for a *meadóg* and not get one." This shorter skean or *miodóg* was thus easily hidden and could in fact be used as a missile weapon. In chapter 3, "Fighting Techniques," we will explore a couple of recorded instances of the skean being flung, dating to 1600 and 1644, respectively. This would have been impossible with the longer variety of skean, the *scian fada*, which could have a blade up to 22" in length.

LONG SKEAN, OR *SCIAN FADA*

In 1518, Laurent Vital, a Burgundian secretary to the Imperial Archduke Ferdinand, made a forced landing at Kinsale. Vital says of the Gaelic Irish, "They have at their belts very dangerous weapons, after the manner of poignards with three edges having a handle like a bread knife of which the blade is more than an ell long."[31] At this date, Vital may well be using the original measure of an ell, which was from the elbow to the tip of the middle finger, about 18". John Derricke in his *Image of Ireland* (1581) says, "A foyner of three quarters of a yarde long, is the Woodkarnes knife." *Foyne* meant to stab. For instance, the State Papers record the death of Edmond Tyrrye on August 27, 1548, who was "murdrede by 23 foynes of an Irishe knyffe, geven hym in to the very hart."[32] Later in his book, Derrricke adds, "Long stabbers pluck thei forthe, in steede of handsome knives."[33] An anonymous Spanish account of the Irish in 1579 says, "The knives that are used at table are so long, that they exceed even their daggers in size."[34]

This longer variety of skean figures in the *Calendar of Ormond Deeds*, where in 1557, Dame Joan, Countess of Ormond and Ossory, must restore "three long knives, six shirts, etc." stolen by her servants, and in 1558 several Butler kern are accused of stealing "2 long knives" from William Oge Fanning.[35] "Long-skeanes" are listed among the arms of idle kerns required to surrender their weapons in 1604 after Tyrone's Rebellion (see page 18). A 1624 proclamation reads: "No man to wear after 1 August next any mantles, trowses, or long skeines. . . . Sheriffs to break long skeines, and to take off and cut to pieces any mantles or trowses worn in public."[36]

Knowledge of the long skean was preserved in folklore recorded in the nineteenth century, but referring to events of the previous century. Thus, a Mayo tale tells of a man who, having safely traversed the wolf-infested passage from Roonith to Drummin, gave his *sgian fada* to a traveler going in the opposite direction, with fatal results on his own return.[37] Also from Mayo, a story is told of the men of the Tiernan family driving off a party that were about to abduct the family's daughter in a "marriage by capture." "When the men entered, taking a *sgian fada* for each of them, [Mrs. Tiernan] armed her husband and sons."[38] According to James Berry in his *Tales of Mayo and Connemara*, this practice of abducting a bride was called "foudagh" (*fhuadach*).[39]

The length of a *scian fada* is specified in the Irish poem "Pléaraca na Ruarach" ("O'Rourke's Feast"), "englished" by Dean Jonathan Swift in 1720 from MacGuaran's original, and celebrating the sixteenth-century chief Brian na Murtha O'Rourke.[40]

> They rise from their feast, and hot are their brains,
> a cubit at least, the length of their skeans.

As noted above, a cubit is generally considered to be 18" but varied from 17" to 22", being roughly reckoned as a man's arm length from his elbow to the tip of the middle finger.

LATE SURVIVAL OF THE SKEIN

Among the traditional Gaelic Irish soldiery, the skean was particularly associated with the kern, but John Dymmok (1600), for one, gives his Irish horseman "a sword, a skein and a spear," while his galloglass has "a shirt of mail, a scull and a skein."[41] Use of the skean survived the transition to modern weaponry among the native Irish in the last decade of the sixteenth century. In 1594, a detached force of Tyrone's modernized army had 400 shot, 180 pike, 200 horse, and "two hundred churls with darts and skeins."[42] But the new Irish troops, the bonnaughts, armed with firearms and pikes, also continued to carry the skean. In 1600, O'More's bonnaught pikemen carried them, as discussed in chapter 3, "Fighting Techniques." And a force of Connacht bonnaughts defeated in Munster in 1601 lost "150 pikes and peeces, besides many swords, targets and skeans."[43]

The conclusion of Tyrone's Rebellion left many "idle swordsmen" without employ, and Sir Arthur Chichester published a *Proclamation for Disarminge of Kerns* in February 1604, requiring all weapons be turned in by "many idle kern . . . being armed with swords, targetts, pikes, shot, headpieces,

Fig. 7. "Irish Skein." Rare woodcut from Harbillon's *Costume in England*, 1885, p. 367. Note the thick back of the blade, rudimentary guard, and grip, apparently of antler (but see the "dadagh" below). *PD-US-expired*

Fig 8. Detail from "Dravn after the Qvicke" (i.e., from life), a woodcut in the Ashmolean Museum, Oxford, shows an Irish kern who took part in Henry VIII's invasion of France in 1544. The kern brandishes a skean overhead with an ice-pick grip. The blade is about 22" in length, exceeding the length of the man's own forearm. Note thick back of the blade. *Image © Ashmolean Museum, University of Oxford*

Fig. 9. "The knives that are used at table are so long, that they exceed even their daggers in size." From Derricke's *Image of Ireland* (1581). *Wikimedia Common*

Fig.10. "A foyner of three quarters of a yarde long, is the Woodkarne's knife." From Derricke's *Image of Ireland* (1581). *Wikimedia Commons*

Fig. 11. Kern with darts, targe, and short skean with antler (?) handle. After an Ulster map of 1600 in Lambeth Palace Library.

horsemen's-staves, long-skeanes."[44] But unrest continued, and in 1635 William Brereton passed through Morgan Kavanagh's woods, where lurked "sixteen stout rebels . . . every one of them with his pistols, skene, and darts."[45] The skean is ubiquitous in notices of the Irish uprising after 1641, and as late as February 1653, Martha Love "saith, that the town [Galway] was full of Ireconnaught rogues, in their trowses and broages, all armed with pikes, skeans, and swords."[46]

In 1690, the famous siege of Castle Moret took place in County Laois. In his memoirs, Jonah Barrington recounted that his grandaunt, Elizabeth Fitzgerald, found herself surrounded in the castle by the O'Cahills of Timahoe. She survived the siege but lost her husband, whereupon the local squires plotted who should take her as wife in a marriage by capture. These squires, having collected at Castle Reban, drew lots, and the winner, M'Carthy O'Moore, was assured the assistance of the others. But Elizabeth learned of their plans and sent the ward of Castle Moret on a preemptive strike: "Every man took his long skeen in his belt—had a thick club, with a strong spike at the end of it, slung with a stout leather thong to his wrist; and under his coat, a sharp broad hatchet with a black blade and a crooked handle. And thus, in silence, the twenty-five Moret warders, commanded by Keeran Karry, set out with their priest, the piper, and the gossoon [servant boy] with a copper pot slung over his shoulders as a drum." Proceeding to Castle Reban, the ward arrived at midnight to the sounds of the inmates "practising at the sword or skeen." Drawing the inmates out by a ruse, the warders set upon them with loud cries of "A Gerald!" accompanying each "crash of the murderous hatchet, or every plunge of the broad-bladed skeen." Elizabeth's ward prevailed, and with the daylight "M'Carthy O'Moore was discovered in the farm-yard, with nearly all his face sliced off, and several skeen wounds in his arms and body."[47]

There is, indeed, evidence that the skean remained in use right into the eighteenth century. John Dunton, describing the rapparees in 1698, says, "Their arms, like those of the old Irish Kearns, were a half pike and a skeane."[48] And William Moffett, whose *Hesperi-neso-graphia* was printed in 1724, says of his hero the Irishman Gillo:[49]

With a skean he'd stab and charge about,
and often let the blood come out.

As we saw above in the section on the history of the long skean, there is evidence from folklore that the *scian fada* was being used in remote County Mayo into the eighteenth century, since it features in folklore recorded there in the nineteenth century. These tales feature the *scian fada* being used for self-defense against wolves and suitors.

The skean saw a rather less savory use when in September 1741, the scandalous Bodkin murders took place at Carnbane, County Galway. The son of landowner Oliver Bodkin found himself usurped in his father's will by a new son from a second marriage and sought revenge against his father, stepmother, and their new son and heir. He met to plot with several associates, including his uncle Dominick, and one of the company produced a penknife. "Dominick, who was a judge of weapons, objected that it would not answer, and brought out two long keen Irish skenes, which he said he would retouch upon the grindstone." On the appointed night, the conspirators first dispatched the family servants, who were found sleeping in a barn: "A few minutes later the skenes were across their throats." They then proceeded to the family asleep in the house. After a brief trial at the Galway Assizes, all faced the hangman.[50]

Fig. 12. Sir Neil O'Neill and his kern (1680), by Michael Wright. *Photo: Tate*

Fig. 13. Sir Neil's skean handle, carved in baroque style. *Photo: Tate*

Fig. 14. Kern's skean, with spiral carved handle, similar byknife, plain scabbard. *Photo: Tate*

Fig. 15. Sir Neil's skean, scabbard with bronze locket, and chape of bronze wire. *Photo: Tate*

CHAPTER 2

MANUFACTURE AND POSSIBLE EXPORT OF THE SKEAN

In the Tudor era, sword blades made in specialist centers—usually in Germany—were among the goods traded into Gaelic Ireland by the Spanish and French fishing fleets that arrived annually on the southwest coasts. Irish smiths would then add distinctive sword hilts to the blades.[1] Skeans, however, were made locally in their entirety by Irish smiths. In depositions after the Irish uprising of 1641, John Goldsmith recalled the month of July that year, "when this deponent observed that certain Irish smiths had in a short space of time made a multitude of skeans, whereby he conceived that soome sudden mischief and insurrection would then ere long ensue."[2]

In 1611 Sir Thomas Phillips proposed a scheme for plantation in "the county of Colerane and the Derry," including an ironworks, "for the Irish of themselves wil take the ore, and in short time make iron; and it proves to be very good of which they make their skeynes and darts."[3]

Bronze soldering and plating appears to have been a characteristic technique of Gaelic Irish smiths. The barbed dart heads seen in John Michael Wright's portrait of Sir Neil O'Neill (fig. 16, *right*), are evidently plated with bronze, possibly meant to prevent rust. Etienne Rynne noted that bronze plating on sixteenth-century Gaelic Irish sword hilts and skean handle fittings—an unusual technique—may have been a Gaelic cultural marker: "The use of copper, brass or bronze to solder and/or plate iron is apparently not widespread, but is known from some Irish weapons, including the hilts of sixteenth[-]century swords, and also some arrowheads, and it is probably justified to regard it as an Irish technique of sixteenth[-]century date."[4]

Gaelic Irish ironworking retained other distinct characteristics through the Tudor era. While their iron-smelting furnaces were of the slag-tapping variety common to Europe, the Gaelic Irish maintained the practice of floor-level smithing in their forges. Waist-level smithing had been adopted elsewhere from the fourteenth century on. Also, whereas urban smiths in areas of English cultural influence within Ireland were practicing waist-level smithing using iron tuyeres (nozzles) to separate their bellows from the forge, it was a Gaelic cultural marker to retain the use of ceramic tuyeres. Rural smithies in Gaelic Ireland were circular structures with fireproof mud walls and tended to be isolated from areas of habitation.[5]

Fig. 16. Sir Neil O'Neill's dart head, seen in the center of this detail, is plated with bronze, a Gaelic Irish smithing technique. *Photo: Tate*

The sixteenth-century Gaelic Irish smith had rights to the heads of cattle slaughtered locally, a tradition that continued into the nineteenth century. In folklore, the ironworker had a reputation as a potentially malevolent, liminal character with mysterious powers to transmute matter from one state to another. Wariness of smiths is reflected in an eighth-century hymn for protection from the "spells of women, smiths and druids."[6] Captain De Cuéllar was a survivor of the Spanish Armada shipwrecked on the coast of Sligo in 1588, and his account calls to mind these old associations. He describes his temporary enslavement by a "wicked, savage blacksmith," a Gaelic Irish smith who pursued his trade in a "deserted valley." This is thought to have been in Glenade Valley in County Leitrim. There, De Cuéllar was forced to work the bellows and endure the smith's wife, "an accursed old woman," until rescued by a passing priest.[7]

There is evidence that the skean was exported to Tudor England, at least in small quantities. The Bristol Port Books record knives of all descriptions being imported from England into the anglicized urban centers of southeast Ireland in large numbers during the sixteenth century. But the same source also shows knives being exported from Ireland to Bristol in two separate instances in the year 1526. It seems a reasonable inference that these were skeans, and perhaps due to the elaborately carved handles and sheaths, they were relatively expensive, valued at 3s 4d and 6s 8d apiece.[8]

References in contemporaneous English literature certainly indicate that the Irish skean saw occasional use in that country. A manuscript folio dated to the mid-seventeenth century but containing earlier material, *Robin Hood and Guy of Gisborne* (British Library Add MSS 27879), contains these lines:

> Robin pulled forth an Irish knife,
> And nicked Sir Guy in the face.

Robert Green's polemical essay *A Quip for an Upstart Courtier, &c.* (1592) describes "an ill-favoured knave, who wore by his side a skane, like a brewer's bung-knife." Most famously, there is a reference in Shakespeare's *Romeo and Juliet* (1597) in which Juliet's nurse scolds Mercutio: "Scurvy knave! I am none of his skainsmates." The term skainsmate is glossed in E. Cobham Brewer's *Dictionary of Phrase and Fable* as "a dagger-comrade; a fencing-school companion; a fellow cut-throat. Skain is an Irish knife."

Fig. 17. Floor-level smithing, as practiced by Gaelic Irish smiths. Late-seventeenth-century Gondar Homiliary, Ethiopia. *Courtesy of the Walters Art Museum*

Fig. 18. Late medieval clay tuyere from Castleland, Ferns, County Wexford. *Courtesy of P. Rondelez; excavation director: K. McLoughlin*

Fig. 19, *above. Écossais, Chef de Clan*, a lithograph by Devéria. *Courtesy of City of Edinburgh Museums and Art Galleries, Scotland / Bridgeman Images*

Fig. 20, *above. Dravne after the Qvicke*, an anonymous woodcut, ca. 1544. *Image © Ashmolean Museum, University of Oxford*

FIGHTING TECHNIQUES

Fynes Moryson remarked on the Irishman's "dexterity of vsing skeans and Darts,"[1] a skill gained no doubt by "practising at the sword and skeen," as we saw the O'Cahills of Castle Reban doing in Chapter 1. Like the Roman gladius, the skean was frequently worn on the right side. It rested at an angle across the front of the thigh, as indicated by Derricke's woodcuts in his *Image of Ireland* (1581) and the 1680 portrait of Sir Neil O'Neill. As long as the sheath was not too tight, this would allow the skean to be plucked out quickly with the point down, which seems to have been the habitual combat grip, providing more strength than a hammer grip.

The well-known print of Irish kern, titled *Dravne after the Qvicke* and dating to about 1544, depicts two of its subjects quarreling on the right-hand side. One has raised his skean above his head, point down in an ice-pick grip. This is usually interpreted as an offensive posture, but there is evidence from the Highlands that this may also have been employed as a defensive technique.

William Gordon Alexander recalls that Captain C. W. Macdonald of the 93rd Highlanders was his regiment's premier swordsman while serving in India during the Mutiny. Macdonald taught the defensive use of the Highland dirk, "and one day at Bithur he illustrated to me how the Highlanders used to use it, not only as a weapon of offense, using it then with its point turned outwards, but as a shield and buckler to protect the head and the whole body against sword-cuts, with the broad back of the blade pressed against the forearm, point towards the elbow and edge turned outwards, always, of course, using the left hand."[2]

As mentioned above in the section on *miodóga*, the short skean could be used as a missile weapon. The Frenchman M. DeBoullaye LeGouz, visiting Ireland in 1644 during the Wars of the Confederacy, says, "The Irish carry a scquine or Turkish dagger, which they dart very adroitly at 15 paces distance."[3] This is confirmed by an incident in 1600, in which the rebel Owney MacRory O'More had his pikemen seize the Earl of Ormond during a parley. One of the earl's companions on horseback broke free and said later, "We escaped the push of their pikes (which they freely bestowed) and the flinging of their skenes, without any hurt."[4]

According to Archibald MacGregor (*Lecture on the Art of Defense*, 1791), the Scottish Highlanders were also skilled in knife throwing. MacGregor says of the Highland dirk: "It was also used much in the same manner as a lance: for I have been informed that many of those people were dexterous marksmen with it; for they would throw at a considerable distance and hit the object to a certainty."[5] As happened so often, Highland and Irish Gaelic practices echoed one another.

Memory of flinging the skean seems to have survived in folklore. There is a recurring Irish folktale, of which more than 150 versions have been collected, called "Knife against the Wave." Usually, a party of fishermen find their boat threatened by a monster wave until one of them flings his skean into it, killing the wave. Later he is led to discover that he has inadvertently injured a fairy woman.[6]

Daggers had grown in importance with the increased use of plate armor during the thirteenth century. As sword and spear became less effective against the new defenses, the dagger was added to the knight's panoply. It was used particularly for grappling, and its strong and narrowly pointed blade was intended to pierce mail and seek out gaps in plate armor.[7]

In the section on "Origins" in chapter 1, we noted that the skean blades bear a greater resemblance to the blades of certain ballock and rondel daggers than they do to those of the earlier seax. The skean's blade was invariably stiff and thick backed, with a sharply tapered profile. This is the sort of blade most commonly found on later rondel daggers, and many ballock daggers as well.

Fig. 21. Hans Talhoffer's Fechtbusch, 1467. Fighting with rondels, demonstrating possible attacks and defense. *Wikimedia Commons*

A nineteenth-century writer tells us "The skeon-fadd, or long knife ... was used by the Irish when in short holds."[8] For instance, at the battle of Clontibret in 1595, the rebel Earl of Tyrone was attacked by a giant Palesman named Seagrave, and they shivered their lances on one another. Seagrave then wrestled Tyrone out of his saddle, and they both fell grappling to the ground. Tyrone dispatched his enemy with a knife thrust under skirt of his mail shirt. The knife used was likely a skean.[9]

As with the rondel dagger, the pommel end of the skean is invariably flat, so that the palm of the free hand could be applied to it to increase the force of a downward thrust. Both were designed as stabbing weapons, with cutting being of only secondary concern.

The fully developed rondel dagger has its handle enclosed by circular plates at either end, making it easy for an armored man with obscured vision to locate and grip it. The skean is notable for having no guard, but all the surviving handles are deeply carved with patterns of interlace in the form of a Saint Andrew's cross, or in a spiral or barley twist. This would have given a very firm grip and assisted with blade alignment. The spiral carving was very common on the grips of rondel daggers.

The overhead blow using the ice-pick grip, as illustrated in Talhoffer's manuscript at left, is the most instinctual and common way of striking with a knife. It is also the most effective grip, and medieval fight manuals clearly favor it. There also exist a number of very long rondel daggers, comparable in size to the *scian fada*, some of which are in the Royal Armouries (*right*). These would have presumably been used more like a short sword. Thus we can say that, like the Scottish Highland dirk, the Irish skean was an essentially medieval weapon in design and function, which survived well into the Early Modern period.

Fig. 22. Long single-edged rondel dagger, 1400–1434. Overall length, 20"; blade 15" long. *Courtesy of Royal Armouries Museum*

MORPHOLOGY AND SHEATHS

HANDLE TYPOLOGY

Two kinds of wooden handle are found on surviving skeans. First is the spirally carved barley twist, of flattened cylindrical section, as found on the Corbally *scian fada* (fig. 24, *opposite*), and the River Corrib skean (fig. 77, page 59). This spiral-grooved handle is also seen on Sir Neil O'Neill's kern in Wright's painting from 1680 (fig. 14, page 19), and in Derricke's illustrations of kerns from 1581 (fig. 26, *opposite*).

The second kind of handle is elegantly waisted, carved with crossed bands of Gaelic revival three-strand plait knot work, and of flattened oval section (fig. 25, *opposite*). One of the bands forming the cross is staggered where it passes under the other. This variety is found on the surviving handles from Tonybaun and Athlone and is implied by the iron remains from Ballycolliton. It is thus limited to short skeans, or *miodóga*, among surviving examples, though the handle of Sir Neil O'Neill's long skean (fig. 13, page 19) bears a superficial resemblance in the crossed legs of the baroque-style mythological figure, possibly Typhon, carved on it.

SKEAN SHEATHS

A poem from 1359, "Cathreim Thoirdhealbhaigh" ("The Triumphs of Turlough"), describes a "smooth belt that in cunningly wrought sheath carried his deadly skean."[1] The use of tooled decoration of "Opus Hibernicum" on the sheaths of skeans is indicated by the following description

Fig. 23. Typhon by Wenceslaus Hollar, about 1650. Might this be the character carved on Sir Neil O'Neill's skean handle? *Wikimedia Commons*

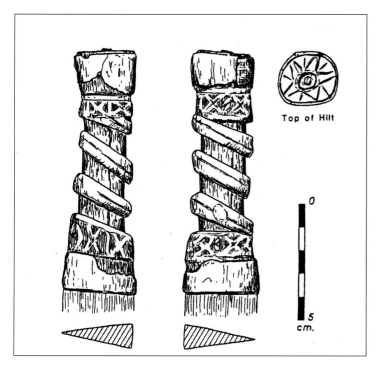

Fig. 24, Spiral-carved skean handle of cylindrical shape, from Corbally. *Courtesy of the Thomond Archaeological Society*

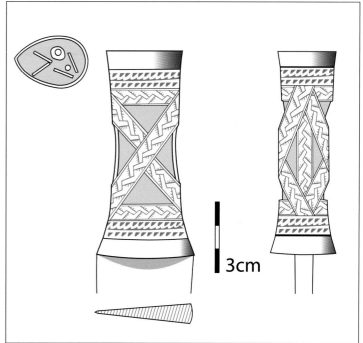

Fig. 25, Elegantly waisted ovoid section handle with interlace carving. *Restored skean handle from Tonybaun*

Fig. 26, *left*: Kerns from Derricke's *Image of Ireland* (1581). They carry long skeans with spiral-carved handles like the one pictured above from Corbally. The recess of the spiraling groove is indicated by cross-hatching in the woodcut.

The sheaths of Derricke's skeans invariably terminate in a ribbed chape, formed of brass wire wound around the last 3" of the sheath. Such a chape was discovered with the Corbally skean but subsequently lost (fig. 42, page 35). It can also be seen in fig. 15, page 19, above.

The manner of suspension is identical to that seen in Wright's portrait of Neil O'Neill (page 19, *above*), the skean being worn "point blanke at his codpiece," at an angle across the right thigh. Skeans are often seen on lanyards around the neck, and in Wright's painting they are worn thus, but underneath the jacket. This may be the case with Derricke as well. *Wikimedia Commons*

of the leather cover of the Cup of Saint Malachy, written by Fr. Patrick Fleming in 1623 and thus providing a terminus ante quem for their use: "Its cover is more precious than itself, being of leather wonderfully embossed and adorned with intertwinings according to the Irish style, of singular ornamentation generally used on the sheaths of oblong knives."[2]

A remarkably perfect leather skean sheath of exactly this description was discovered in a bog at Kilcumber, County Offaly (National Museum reg. no. 1947:286). It would have accommodated the Corbally skean quite well. It is a skilled piece of leatherwork, of single-piece folded-over construction, its seam running along the blade's back.

KICUMBER SHEATH

It is sewn with naturally colored linen thread with a closed seam, stitched grain/flesh in a running stitch, very close to the leather's edges, which are pulled into a subtle wavy pucker. The stitching has about eight awl piercings per inch. The leather of the upper section is molded to take the skean handle, and its mouth is finished with a shallow scallop edge. The sheathed skean was probably worn at an angle across the right thigh, as in Derricke's woodcuts and the painting of Sir Neil O'Neill.

The front face is decorated with a panel of tightly woven, four-strand plait knot work. Etienne Rynne felt this dated it to the sixteenth century. The back has a panel of simpler design in a stepped pattern, while the handle portion has interwoven St. Andrew's cross designs, simpler on the back than on the front. A narrow horizontal band of stepped or "key" pattern separates the upper or handle section from the lower or blade section. Most of the deeply incised basic shapes are filled in with finer, faintly incised hatching. There are six or seven strands of this infill on the bands forming the St. Andrew's crosses, and four on the knot work and stepped bands along the blade section, reducing to three as the pattern tightens.

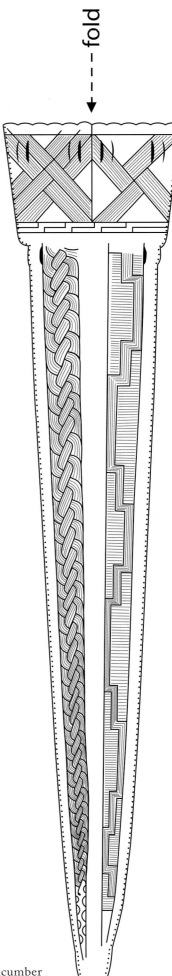

Fig. 27. Kilcumber sheath pattern

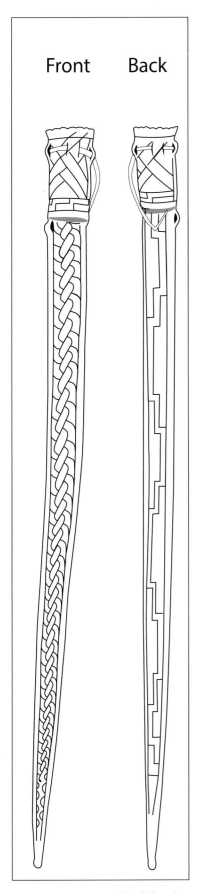

Fig. 28, Line drawing of the Kilcumber sheath

Fig. 29. Kilcumber sheath from the front

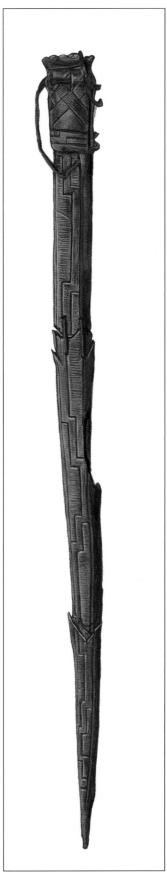

Fig. 30. Kilcumber sheath from the back

Fig. 31, Views of the top of the Kilcumber sheath, molded into a cup to take the handle. *From left to right*: view with blade edge toward viewer; view of front panel; view of back panel; view of stitching edge along the broad back of the blade (upper portion of sheath is without its stitching, which must have broken off with a portion of the adjacent leather).

Fig. 32, Views of Kilcumber sheath, showing incised decoration, the fine tip, and the seam, with detail of stitching along the broad back of the skean

The upper section has vertical cuts just below the scalloped edge to form four evenly spaced loops to take a suspension thong. Just below the upper section, there are two cuts at the outer edges of the incised panels to form a similar loop.

The leather is rather thick, nearly a ¼", and the stitched seam is complete from the finely finished tip to about 10" up, after which a narrow strip surrounding what would have been the remaining stitching appears to have broken off from both edges. The mouth of the sheath now measures about 5" around, and the cup formed by the upper section of the sheath is 3" deep and now measures 4" around at its base at the narrow band of stepped pattern. The decorative panels are about an inch across at their widest, with plain borders of a ½" framing them on either side. The sheath is 23½" long, and a suggested pattern is shown in Fig. 27.

EDINBURGH SHEATH

A second complete skean sheath accompanies the Edinburgh skean (page 60, *below*). This sheath is a very close parallel to the single-piece construction of the Kilcumber sheath, with the top few inches again molded to take the handle, and stitching up one side only.

The front face is decorated with a panel of loosely woven, four-strand plait knot work. The back has a panel of more complex design, with three connected rows of two-strand plait descending in parallel and periodically interconnecting. The handle portion again has interwoven St. Andrew's cross designs. Lightly incised hatching is again employed, here mostly as background fill under the ribbons of interlace, but also to give dimensionality to the interwoven St. Andrew's cross figure.

The execution is not as carefully done as that on the Kilcumber sheath, with ribbons of interlace sometimes going astray, but the sheath has its own vigorous appeal. A notable feature is the use of rows of Vandyke or zigzag tooling to frame off areas.

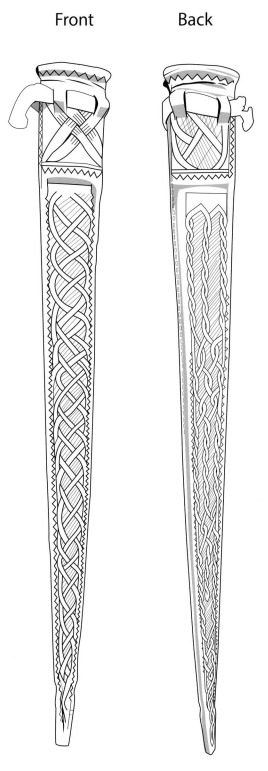

Front   Back

Fig. 33. Line drawing of the Edinburgh sheath, preserving flaws in the very loose four-strand plait interlace, a pattern that recurs on the horizontal bands of carving on the skean's handle.

Fig. 34: Views of the top of the sheath, molded into a cup to take the handle. *From left to right*: view of blade edge (note that the blade has cut the leather near the mouth of the sheath); view of front panel; view of back panel; view of stitching along the broad back edge of the blade. *Courtesy of David Oliver*

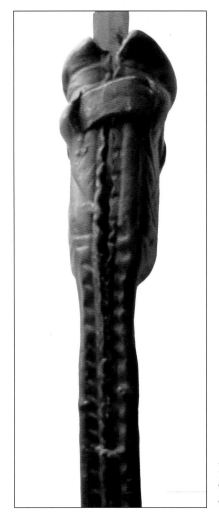

Fig. 35: The seam, showing zigzag tooling on either side of the stitching all the way down. *Courtesy of David Oliver*

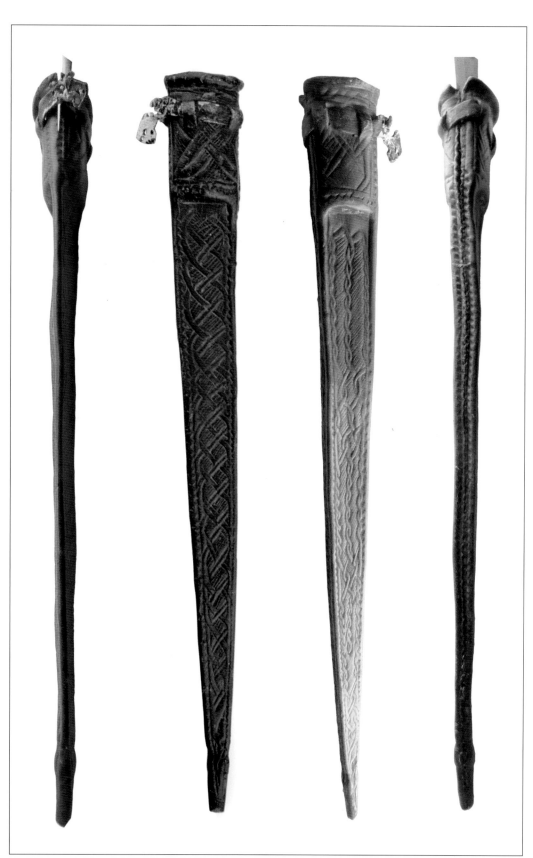

Fig. 36, Sheath with skean in place. *Courtesy of David Oliver*

Fig. 37, Views of sheath, showing, *left to right*: view of blade edge; view of front panel; view of the back panel; view of the stitching on the broad back edge of the blade—rows of zigzag tooling border either side of the stitching for its whole length. *Courtesy of David Oliver*

The leather sheath of O'Donovan's sixteenth-century "dadagh" is tooled with a simpler ladder and zigzag pattern (fig. 45, page 39, *below*). Like the Kilcumber and Edinburgh *sciana fada* sheaths, that of the dadagh is without any metal fittings.

One of Derricke's best woodcuts depicts a battle with a fallen Irish horseman in the foreground. The scabbard of his sword has a short skean attached to it, the sheath of which is incorporated into the sword's scabbard in the manner of a "byknife." This is a medieval fashion, seen in Scottish dirks to this day, with knife—and sometimes fork also—being carried in separate sheaths or pockets built into the outside of the dirk sheath.

Wright's 1680 painting of the Jacobite colonel Neil O'Neill, attired in traditional Irish dress, has the subject's skean suspended precisely as seen in Derricke's woodcuts of one hundred years earlier (page 19, *above*). The narrow baldric is looped around the sitter's neck, and its ends are fitted to the sheath such that the skean lies at an angle across the right thigh, rather than straight up and down. The strap is decorated with three rows of thickset brass studs and appears to be worn beneath the open jacket. The sheath is of plain, dark leather and is finished with a chape of wound bronze wire. There is a faceted bronze locket at the throat of the sheath.

The sheaths of Derricke's skeans invariably terminate in a ribbed chape, formed of bronze wire wound around the last 3" or so of the sheaths. This is not conjecture. It is seen far more clearly in the aforementioned portrait of Sir Neil O'Neill. Such a wire chape was found with the Corbally *scian fada* and survived long enough to be sketched (fig. 42, *opposite page*).

The skean worn by Wright's attendant kern has a dark leather sheath with no chape or locket. There is a small byknife with a wooden handle, much as in a Highland dirk, on the outside of the kern's sheath. His skean has a spiral-carved wooden handle, and the byknife appears to match it.

The blade of what Etienne Rynne called a "baselard knife" was discovered in the river Corrib near Galway city in 1979.[3] It had a byknife corroded to the blade (fig. 40, *opposite page*). The small byknife had an openwork brass handle, indicating a fifteenth-century date. The blade is 16⅛" (41 cm) long, with a maximum width of ¾" (1.9 cm). The byknife is 4⁹⁄₁₆" (11.5 cm) long; its brass handle is 2¹³⁄₁₆" (7.2 cm) long, and the opening in it is 1⅛" (2.8 cm) long. While not a Gaelic Irish artifact, the byknife may give an idea of the blade shape of those used on Gaelic skeans, for which this type of knife may have been a model.

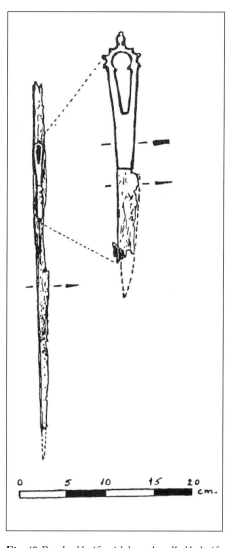

Figs. 38 and 39. Kern ca. 1544. Both the sheath slung by a neck lanyard above, and the one held in the left hand below, show vertical lines, which may indicate a stitching seam. Both sheaths are plain and dark, without fittings. *Left: Photo © Ashmolean Museum, University of Oxford. Right: Photo © Ghent University Library*

Fig. 40. Baselard knife with brass handled byknife in place, from Galway, fifteenth century. *Courtesy of the Galway Archaeological and Historical Society*

Fig. 41. Fallen Irish horseman, with a skean worn in the manner of a "byknife." Isolated detail of the horseman's sword at right for clarity. From Derricke's *Image of Ireland*, 1581. *Wikimedia Commons*

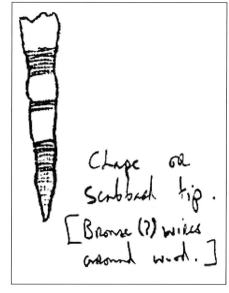

Fig. 42. Bronze wire chape that covered the last 3" of the *scian fada* from Corbally. *Courtesy of the Thomond Archaeological Society*

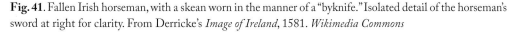

PART B:

THE SURVIVING SKEANS

Sir Neil O'Neill (1680), by
Michael Wright. *Photo: Tate*

CHAPTER 5

SHORT SKEANS, OR *MIODÓGA*

THE DADAGH OF THE O'DONOVAN

This is the one surviving skean with a provenance; the earliest notice of this relic is in Dr. Charles Smith's *Ancient and Present State of the County and City of Cork*, written in 1749.

"The third figure in the following plate represents an ancient Irish weapon, called the Dadahg, in the possession of O'Donovan, of Banlaghan, and preserved as a kind of heir-loom in the family. The drawing is half the size of the original; of this kind are the Durks, used by the Highlanders, and by the Spanish Miquelets to this day; from whom, it is said our Milesian Irish had them, and gave them to the Scots." To which Smith adds this footnote:

"This instrument was taken by the ancestor of O'Donovan, from one of the Clancarty family, in the following manner: Clancarty, Mac Carty Reagh, and O'Donovan, having joined their forces, went into the country of Limerick to plunder, as was the custom of former times; they brought a considerable prey to the castle of Blarney, the seat of Clancarty, who was for having all the cattle drove into his own bawn, without sharing the spoil; and in this manner he had served Mac Carty Reagh before, who then lived at the castle of Kilbritton, and who, on this occasion, called upon O'Donovan to join him that he might assist him, if Clancarty did not share the booty. O'Donovan immediately opposed the driving in of the cattle without dividing them; whereupon, a contest ensued. Clancarty being thrown down by O'Donovan,

with this instrument drawn, intended to kill his antagonist; but O'Donovan perceiving his design, wrenched it from him, with it slew Clancarty on the spot, and divided the spoil with Mac Carty Reagh. It is not certainly known when this happened; but the instrument with this tradition relating to it, is time out of mind preserved in the family." In 1881, O'Donovan of Lissard exhibited "the dadagh, or Irish skean, with which his ancestor slew Clancarty, in the vicinity of Blarney Castle, about 1559."[1]

"The dadagh was 10¼" in length; handle, without guard, 4⅛"; sheath 11¼"; breadth at hilt 1¼"." Dr. Smith's comparison to the Scottish dirk above indicates it had a single edge with a thick back.[2]

The dadagh was featured in the magazine *Ireland of the Welcomes* (vol. 44, no. 3, May/June 1995), which profiled the late O'Donovan of Hollybrook House, who then had the skean mounted on a wall (fig. 45, page 39). The antler handle is very reminiscent of those shown in Harbillon's illustration (fig. 7: the source for this may have been Smith's 1749 drawing of the *dadagh*, however), and in an illustration of an Irish kern on a map of Ulster drawn in 1600 (fig. 11). All three bear some resemblance to the deer antler hafts of certain old Scottish dirks. Etienne Rynne would probably have excluded this weapon from his skean typology, due to the presence of the cross guard. However, the second of two skeans from County Carlow (fig. 101, page 74) shows that the dadagh was not an isolated example.

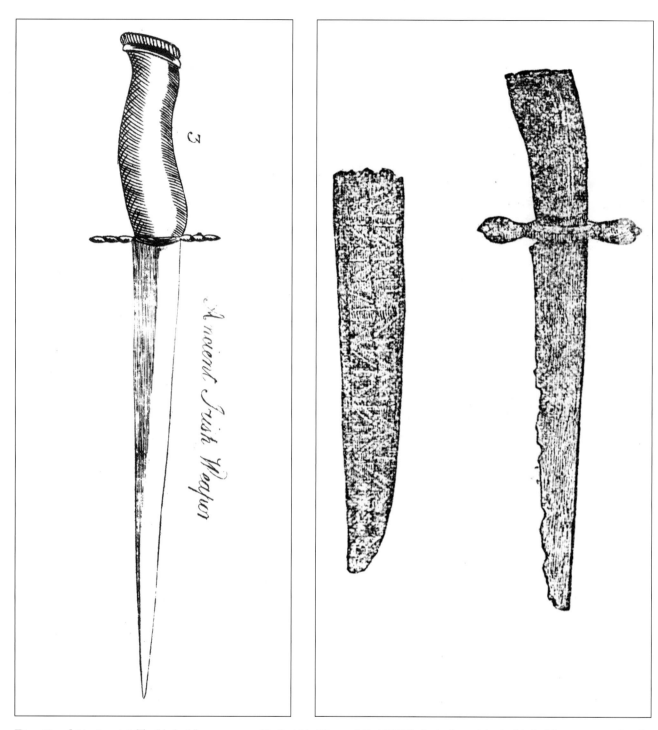

Figs. 43 and 44, *above left*: The "dadagh" as represented in Smith's *History of Cork* (1749). And, *above right*: the "dadagh" as represented in the *Journal of the Royal Historical and Archaeological Association of Ireland* (1881). Smith's illustration may be the source of the image from Harbillon reproduced in fig. 7 on page 17 above. Neither of the above images reflects very well on the accuracy of the artists. *PD–US–expired*

Fig. 45 The "dadagh" as it appeared in 1995, giving a much clearer indication of its actual appearance

BALLYCOLLITON SKEAN

National Museum reg. no. S.A. 1901:30, found during drainage operations at Ballycolliton, County Tipperrary. This is the first of a group of four finds published by Etienne Rynne in 1969 and 1986. I will summarize his descriptions, adding personal observations made at the National Museum in August 2019.

The Ballycolliton find is the best-preserved set of iron pertaining to an excavated skean. While the handle is now missing, the ferrules imply that it was of a type with the skeans from Tonybaun and Athlone. It was discovered 5 feet below the turf, alongside the skeleton of a man and a horse (Rynne notes a similar assemblage of iron dagger, man, and horse was discovered in Kildare in 1859).[3]

The trapezoidal tang is 3⅜" (8.5 cm) long, minus the bent-over tip. The lost wooden handle was secured by an iron nut slipped over the protruding end of the tang and countersunk in the top of the wooden handle, with the tip of the tang then hammered over. The blade is 9⁹⁄₁₆" (24.5 cm) long, and 1⅝" (4.2 cm) wide at the shoulders. Overall length nearly 13" (33 cm). The back of the blade is flat to the length of 1" (2.3 cm) below the shoulders, after which it is faintly faceted longitudinally.

The ferrules are rather thin iron strips, with their ends soldered together in line with the knife's edge. The copper alloy used for soldering was also used to plate the exterior of the ferrules. The lower ferrule has a shallow groove in its underside, where it fitted over the shoulder of the blade. The ferrule's inner edges are as thin as the edge of a butter knife, thickening to ¹⁄₁₆" (1.6 mm) on their outer edges. The lower ferrule has a ⅛" (3.1 mm) flange on its outer edge. The lower ferrule is 1⅝" (4.2 cm) by 1⅛" (2.9 cm) externally, and ⅜" (1 cm) wide. The upper ferrule is 1⁷⁄₁₆" (3.7 cm) by 1³⁄₁₆" (3.1 cm) externally, and ⁵⁄₁₆" (8 mm) wide.

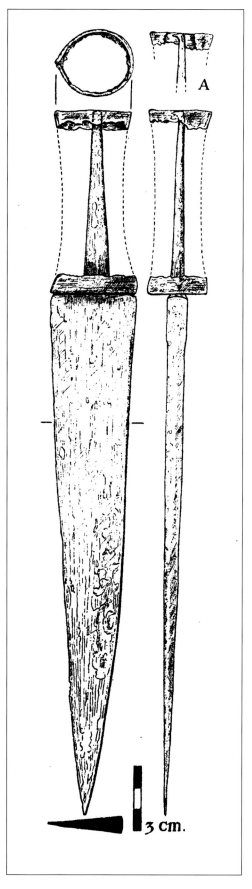

Fig. 46. Ballycolliton skean. After Rynne. *Courtesy of the Thomond Archaeological Society*

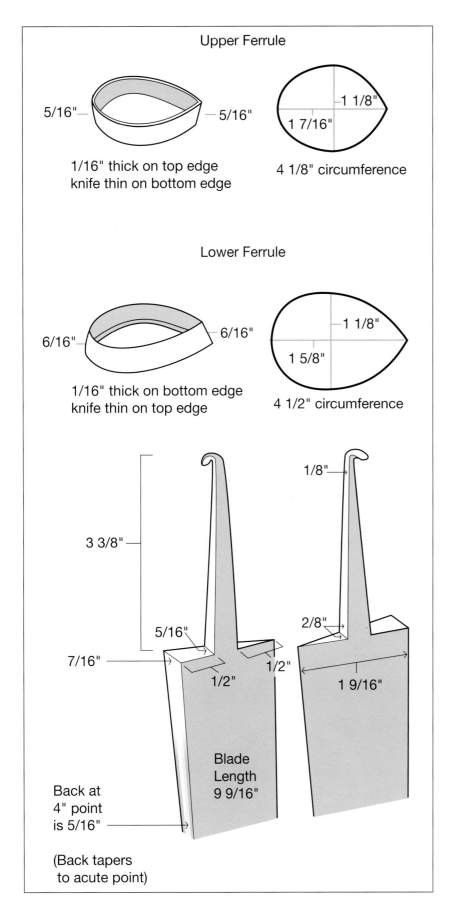

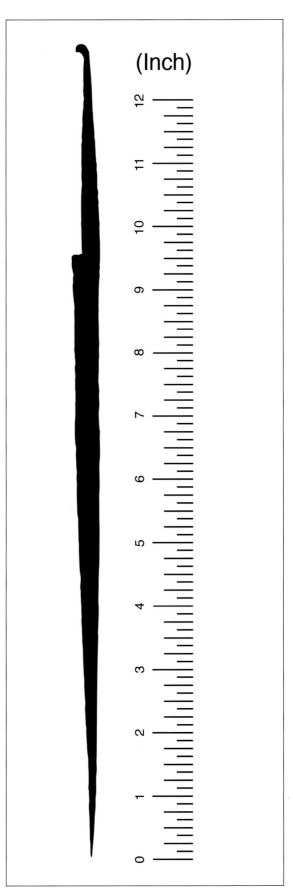

Upper Ferrule

5/16" — — 5/16"

1/16" thick on top edge
knife thin on bottom edge

— 1 1/8"

1 7/16"

4 1/8" circumference

Lower Ferrule

6/16" — — 6/16"

1/16" thick on bottom edge
knife thin on top edge

— 1 1/8"

1 5/8"

4 1/2" circumference

1/8"

3 3/8"

5/16"

7/16"

1/2"

1/2"

2/8"

1 9/16"

Blade
Length
9 9/16"

Back at
4" point
is 5/16"

(Back tapers
to acute point)

(Inch)

Fig. 47. Measurements of Ballycolliton ferrules and skean

Fig. 48. Backside of Ballycolliton blade

Fig. 49. Outer edges of ferrules from Ballycolliton skean, lower ferrule at left, upper ferrule at right. Soldered joints at top, in line with knife edge.

Fig. 50. Lower ferrule from Ballycolliton skean, resting on its outer edge with soldered joint to right

Fig. 51. Lower and upper ferrules resting on their inside edges. Lower ferrule with narrow flange, which fitted over the bottom of the handle.

Fig. 52. Lower and upper ferrules resting on their outside edges

Fig. 53. Ferrules and blade

Figs. 54, 55, 56, and 57, *top*: Blade looking down on shoulders, with tang top peened over.

Below: Back of blade, showing taper to point. Longitudinal faceting very faint.

Second from bottom: Back of blade, showing tang with top peened over

Bottom: Blade shoulders and tang with ferrules approximately in place

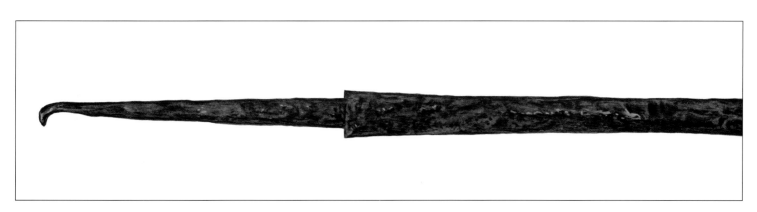

ATHLONE SKEAN

National Museum reg. no. Wk. 36. The second in this series is a wooden handle and partial blade dredged from the river Shannon near Athlone, County Roscommon. The blade is 1⅝" (4.2 cm) wide at the shoulders, and ⁵⁄₁₆" (8 mm) thick at its flat back. It is broken off 5¼" (13.3 cm) below the handle. The handle is of a type with that from Tonybaun but smaller, and with the same style of carving. It is 3⅝" (9.2 cm) in length, 1⅝" (4.12 cm) in width at the base, and 1¼" (3.17 cm) at its top. Overall length is 8⅞" (22.5 cm). My widths for the handle at the base and top are at slight variance with Rynne's.

Rynne notes that the interlace on this handle, while of the same pattern as seen on the Tonybaun skean, is "poorly executed, as if the carver were perfunctorily copying a pattern, and there are bands of deeply cut triangular nicks between the upper and lower bands of interlace and the ferrules."[4] As with the Tonybaun skean, one of the bands forming the saltier is staggered where it crosses beneath the other, so this appears to be intentional. The bottom iron ferrule remains in place, is soldered at front with copper alloy, and was plated overall with the same metal. The tang is riveted into the hilt by a collar of iron wrapped around its end and countersunk into the handle. Four short iron wedges are embedded into the top of the handle, and two into the bottom on either side of the blade. The purpose of the wedges was to make a secure fit for the ferrules.

Rynne noted that the Highland dirk emerges in the second half of the sixteenth century and is the closest parallel to this series of Irish skeans. However, while the skean shares the characteristic of having no cross guard, dirk handles are cylindrical, have haunches reminiscent of ballock or dudgeon daggers, and frequently have a circular brass disc for a pommel cap. The skean handles are not a good match to any of the categories of dirk handles. Rynne says: "Most Highland dirks have finely carved handles covered with interlaced knotwork of multi-strand ribbons, sometimes with the passing of the ribbons below one another accentuated by short incised lines running lengthways from the edges of the uppermost ribbon, just as was done on the Tonybaun handle and was blundered on the Athlone one. This feature seems to the writer, from a general study of Late Medieval interlace in Ireland and Scotland, to belong mainly to the seventeenth and eighteenth centuries. The interlaced art in Ireland as well as in Scotland at this period was, to a large extent, a conscious revival of the Renaissance phase, and not a survival from earlier times. In general, such revived interlace is characterized by its poor quality, its lack of inspiration, and a predominance of simple twists, plait-work, or knotwork, characteristics which are very noticeable in the decoration of the two Irish hilts."

Regarding the use of copper alloy solder and plating, Rynne says: "The use of copper or bronze to solder and/or plate iron is apparently not widespread but is known from some Irish weapons, including the hilts of sixteenth century swords and also some arrowheads, and it is probably justifiable to regard it as an Irish technique of sixteenth[-]century date." He notes that a bifurcate arrowhead of Ward-Perkins type 6 in the National Museum, very similar to one illustrated in Albrecht Durer's 1521 sketch of Irish warriors, is thus treated. And a sixteenth-century Irish sword now on display in the Belfast Museum has its hilt plated with bronze.

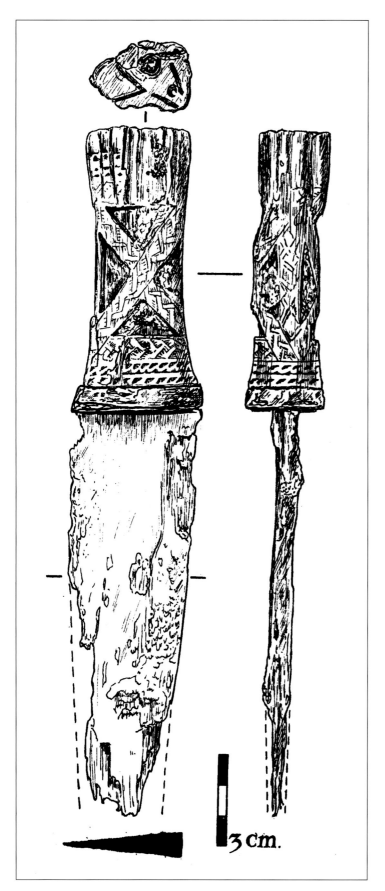

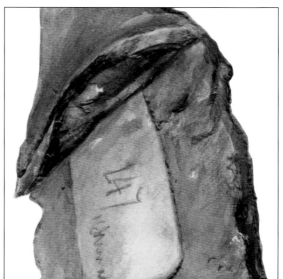

Fig. 58. Wooden skean handle from Athlone, County Galway. After Rynne.
Courtesy of the Thomond Archaeological Society

Figs. 59, 60, and 61, *top*: Pommel end, with iron collar/nut countersunk to take tang
Middle: Underside of handle, with blade edge to left
Bottom: Underside of handle, with blade edge to viewer. Ferrule has narrow flange overlapping the wood of the handle.

Fig. 62, *above*: Four views of the Athlone skean handle, giving full round perspective: *From left to right*: Handle with blade edge facing viewer; handle laid flat with blade edge to left; handle with thick back of blade facing viewer; handle laid flat with blade edge to right.

(*Note*: The staggered arrangement of the saltier arms is reversed or "flipped" on the opposite sides of the handle, as clarified in the sketch at right.)

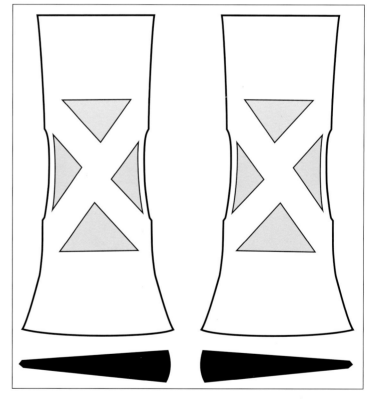

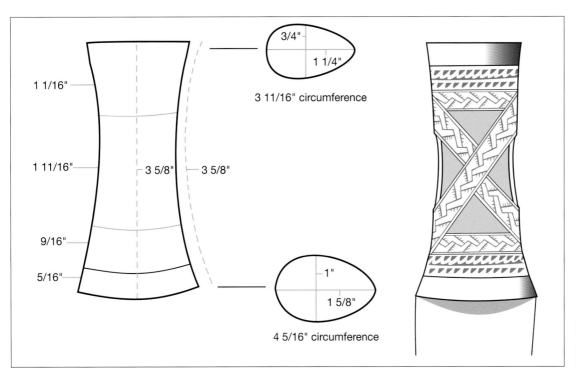

Fig. 63. Measurements of the Athlone skean handle, with reconstructed handle at right

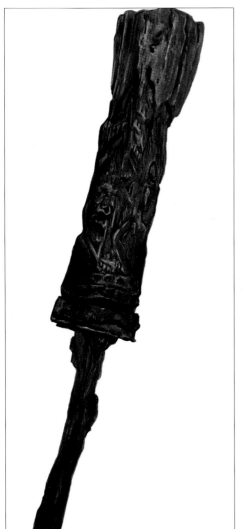

Fig. 64. Backside of handle, showing vertical band of interlace along spine, and the thick back of the blade

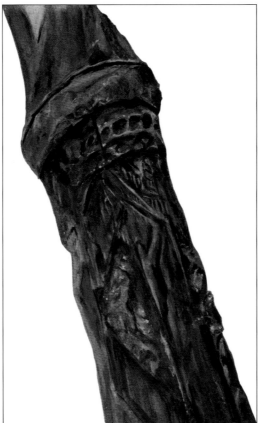

Figs. 65 and 66, *left*: Backside of handle, showing ferrule, two rows of triangular notches, and the end of a diagonal band of interlace overlapping the carved band running on the back spine of the handle.

Right: Handle, with blade edge to left. A narrower vertical band without carving is seen running along the blade edge of the handle front, and the staggered nature of the crossed bands in saltier can be seen.

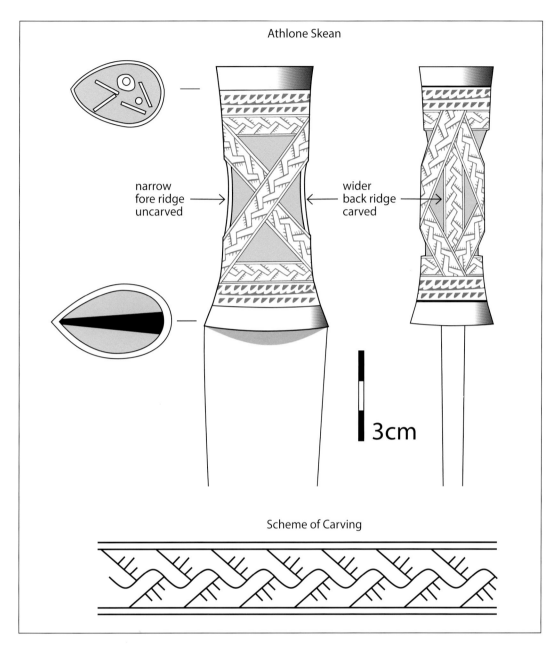

Fig. 67. Athlone skean, restored

TONYBAUN SKEAN

National Museum reg. no. 1966:6. The third in this series is a wooden handle dredged from the Moy at Tonybaun near Ballina, County Mayo.[5] The shoulders of the single-edged blade remain in place in the base of the handle. The blade was about 1¹³⁄₁₆" (4.6 cm) wide at this point and ⅜" (1 cm) thick at the back. There appeared to have been some longitudinal fluting along the back of the blade, giving a beveled effect.

The top and bottom edges of the handle were originally bound with a ferrule of iron, remains of which appear on the top edge. These ferrules were soldered with copper at their angular joint, in line with the knife blade. They were evidently plated overall with copper alloy, and green oxidized remains of copper alloy appear where the top ferrule has gone missing.

Rynne gives the handle measurements: 4½" (11.4 cm) in length, 2⁵⁄₁₆" (5.7 cm) in width at the base, and 1⅜" (3.6 cm) at the top. Rynne's measurement for the handle's top width was slightly wider than mine: 1⁵⁄₁₆" (3.3 cm). The handle was carved overall, but decoration remained on only one side in 1969, having flaked off on the reverse side. The carved decoration consists of two bands of Gaelic revival three-strand plait interlace, crossed to form a St. Andrew's or saltier cross in the center. One of the bands forming the cross is staggered where it crosses beneath the other. This is framed above by a similar band of plaiting running horizontally between the crossed bands and the upper ferrule. All the plaited bands are bordered on both sides by a diagonally hatched frame.

Wherever a ribbon of plait passes under another, this is emphasized by two short incised lines running lengthwise from the edge of the uppermost ribbon. This is seen most clearly in Rynne's reconstruction in fig. 68 at top right. The portion immediately above the lower ferrule is too corroded to determine if it was decorated, but Rynne assumes it originally had a horizontal band of plaiting, as seen below the space for the missing upper ferrule.

Rynne found the "closest parallel" for this series of skeans to be the Highland dirk. They have the same triangular, single-edged blade with square shoulders and a thick back. As we have seen, however, the form of the skean handles is

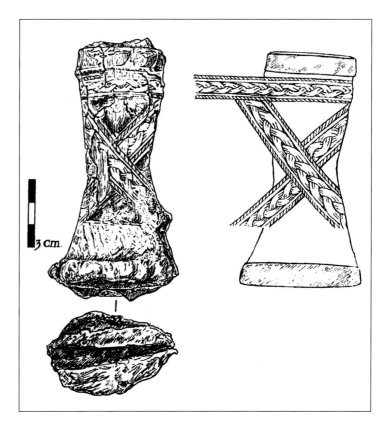

Fig. 68 (from Rynne), *left*: Wooden skean handle from Tonybaun, County Mayo *Right*: Reconstructed drawing of decoration. *Courtesy of the Thomond Archaeological Society*

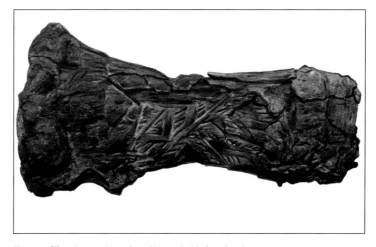

Fig. 69. Tonybaun skean handle, with blade edge lowermost

quite distinct. But Rynne noted the similarity of the interlaced knot work usually found on Highland dirk handles with that on the Tonybaun and Athlone handles from his series of Irish skeans.

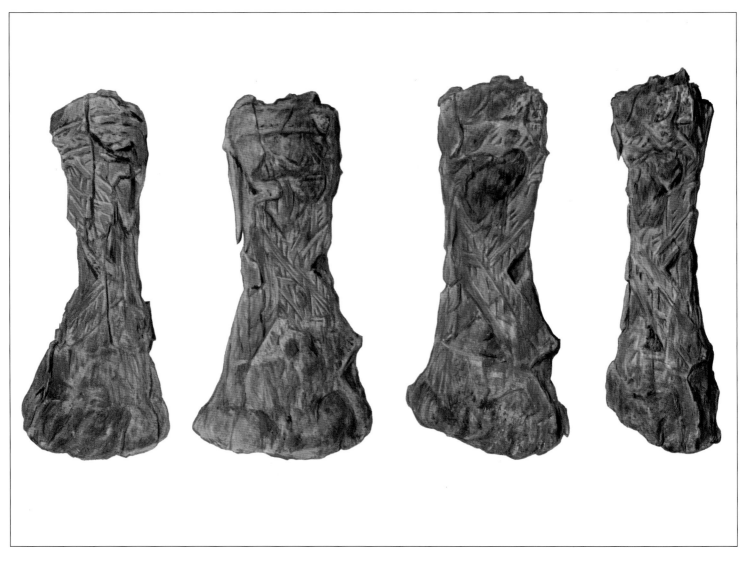

Fig. 70, *above*, *left to right*: Tonybaun skean handle seen from back edge; laid flat with blade edge to right; turned slightly with blade edge coming forward; and last, from blade edge. (*Note*: One side of the handle had its decoration entirely flaked off upon discovery.)

Fig. 71. View of Tonybaun skean handle top along the narrow front side, aligning with the blade edge

Fig. 72. Detail of Tonybaun skean handle top, on the backside, showing horizontal interlace band below ferrule and diagonal interlace band lapping around

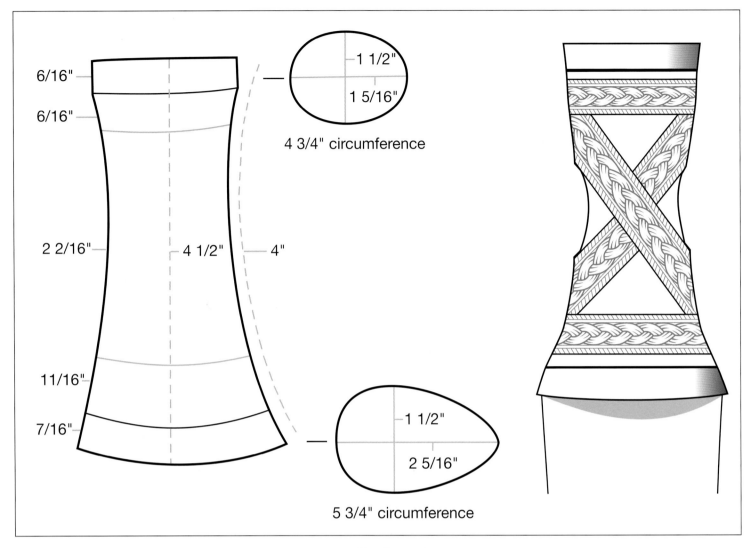

6/16"

6/16"

1 1/2"

1 5/16"

4 3/4" circumference

2 2/16" 4 1/2" 4"

11/16"

7/16"

1 1/2"

2 5/16"

5 3/4" circumference

Fig. 73. Measurements of the Tonbybaun skean handle, with reconstructed handle at right

Fig. 74. Tonybaun skean handle, lower face with remains of blade in place

Fig. 75. Tonybaun skean handle, upper end

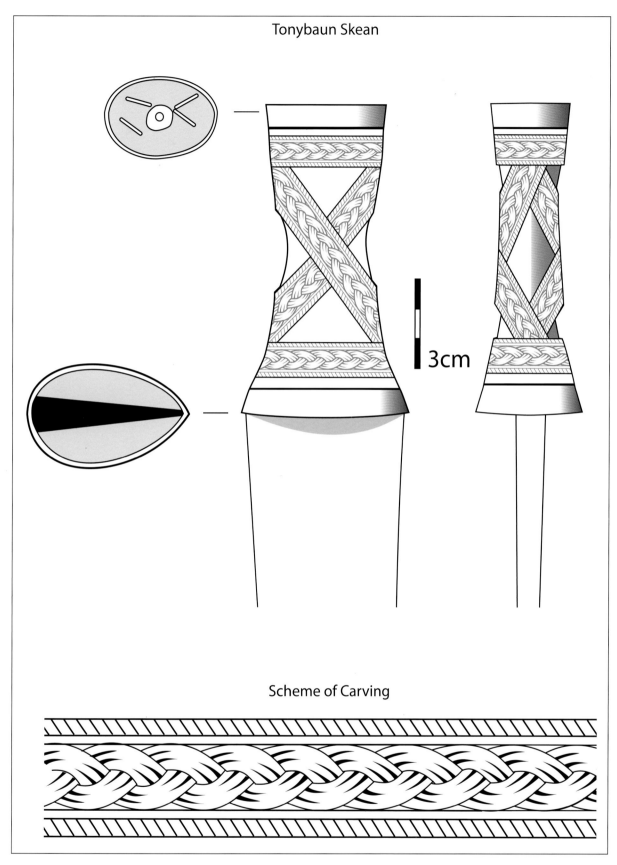

Tonybaun Skean

3cm

Scheme of Carving

Fig. 76. Tonybaun skean, restored

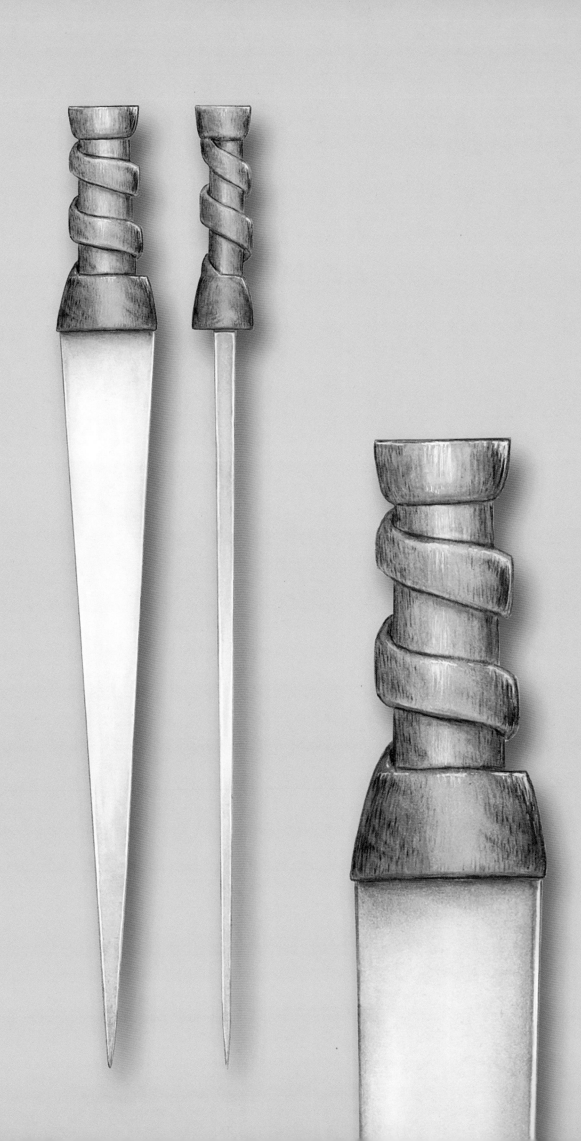

CHAPTER 6

LONG SKEANS, OR *SCIANA FADA*

RIVER CORRIB SKEAN

This skean was found in 1981 by a diver in the river Corrib, in Dangan Lower, near Bushypark, about 2 miles upriver from Galway city.[1] Inquiries were made to the National Museum and the Galway City Museum, but its current whereabouts are unknown. It is a single-edged skean with a wooden handle deeply carved with a spiraling or barley twist pattern. The handle is quite plain and otherwise lacks decoration. However, its discovery made it clear that the *scian fada* from Corbally, which had been found in 1979, was in fact an Irish skean, having a very comparable handle.

The handle was about 4½" long, and the blade about 10½" long, with an overall length approaching 15".

This is the only surviving handle without carved decoration, apart from the spiral or barley twist. It resembles the skean carried by Sir Neil O'Neill's kern (fig. 14) and may reflect the descriptions in chapter 1, "History of the Skean," referring to "a rude wooden handle" and "a handle like a bread knife."

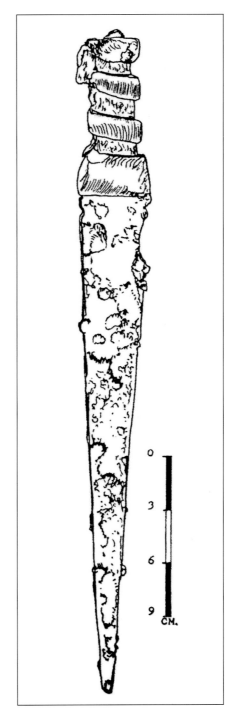

Fig. 77. River Corrib skean. After Rynne.
Courtesy of the Thomond Archaeological Society

EDINBURGH SKEAN

The skean on the following pages was put on auction in Edinburgh in August 2019. It was advertised as a "Rare Scottish Highland Dirk," with the following description: "The blade of triangular section, tapering to a fine point, the back edge engraved 1677, the carved hardwood grip with spiraled grooved and incised borders, the pommel inlaid with geometric steel design and ringed edge; the leather scabbard stitched along the back edge profusely decorated with Celtic knot work and interlace, with remnants of suspension loop. 15¼" (38.8 cm) length of blade, 18⅞" (47.9 cm) overall."

This weapon would be unique among surviving Scottish dirks and doesn't follow the specifications of any known type of dirk. In fact, consultation with a number of specialist collectors of dirks has convinced me that this is in fact a skean.

Atypically for a dirk, but absolutely diagnostic for an Irish skean, it has a waisted handle; iron ferrules about ⅜"+ (1 cm) wide top and bottom, which are tapered inward to accommodate the waisting of the handle; horizontal bands of carved decoration just inside the ferrules; and a diagonal raised band of carved Gaelic revival two-ribbon interlace bordered by a diagonally hatched frame, with surrounding parts excavated out. It combines the Athlone and Tonybaun skeans' diagonal band of interlace with the spiral groove of the Corbally and River Corrib skeans, melding the two styles into one. The sheath is a match to the Kilcumber sheath, the cupped part at top (to take the handle) being similarly incised with an interlaced double-banded saltier, with Gaelic revival interlace in a panel along the blade portion, and again stitched up one side along the thick back of the blade, without metal fittings. And the sheath is cut to make slits for a suspension thong in exactly the same way as the Kilcumber sheath.

Fig. 78. Skean from Edinburgh. *Courtesy of David Oliver*

It is dated 1677 on the back edge of the blade, as with certain Scottish dirks. Stuart-era Gaelic Irish objects are also sometimes dated in this manner, such as the Dalway harp of 1621.

There is a museum accession number painted in white on the handle, so the skean has evidently been in a (regional?) museum collection at some point. The surprisingly late date offers a terminus ante quem for the making of skeans. We can only speculate that it may have been brought back by a veteran of the Williamite War of 1688–1691. But its provenance is unfortunately untraceable, though it has obviously been well cared for. Its condition is consistent with that of the better-preserved Scottish dirks of similar date. In its unexcavated state, it offers a glimpse of the former splendor of the skeans found elsewhere on these pages, which largely have been recovered from underwater.

The recess excavated around the spiral band on the handle begins and ends with a small auricular-style carving shaped like a mouse ear, and then has a single row of eight raised, pointed knobs its full length. The knobs and the other carving are particularly elaborate, and as with the carving on the other skeans' handles, they serve a practical purpose in providing good edge alignment for the user.

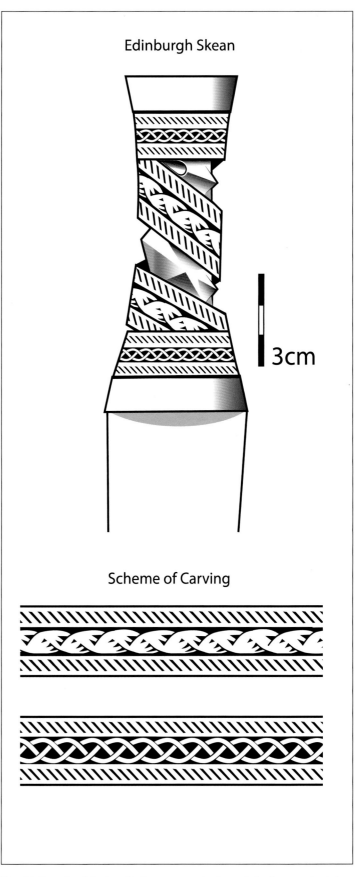

Edinburgh Skean

3cm

Scheme of Carving

Fig. 79, Date engraved on the thick back of the blade, 1⅝" (4.2 cm) from the underside of the grip to the last numeral 7. *Courtesy of David Oliver*

Fig. 80, Details of the handle decoration, which is of a higher standard than that of the sheath

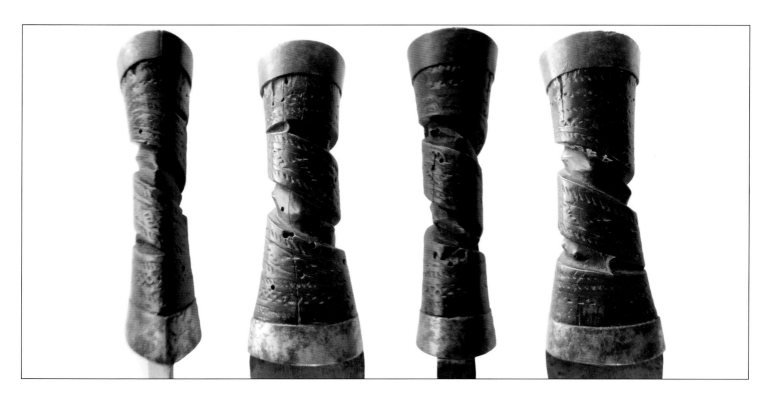

Fig. 81, *above*: Four views of the Edinburgh skean handle, giving full round perspective: *From left to right*, handle with blade edge facing viewer; handle laid flat with blade edge to left; handle with thick back of blade facing viewer; handle laid flat with blade edge to right. *Courtesy of David Oliver*

The carved decoration on the encircling bands consists of Gaelic revival, three-strand plait interlace. All the plaited bands are bordered on both sides by a diagonally hatched frame, which matches the treatment on the Tonybaun skean handle. However, as with the Athlone skean handle, the quality of the interlace carving is decadent.

Note the iron ferrules, particularly the views to the right. The metal flange of the lower ferrule can be seen overlapping the handle, a feature seen on the lower ferrules of the Athlone and Ballycolliton skeans. Rynne also noted of the Ballycolliton skean that "the lower ferrule has a shallow groove in its underside where it fitted over the shoulder of the blade." This is likely the case here as well, judging by the fit of the blade into the ferrule.

The upper ferrule is 1⁷⁄₁₆" (3.4 cm) by 1¼" (3.1 cm) externally, and ⅜"+ (1 cm) wide. The lower ferrule is 1⅜" (3.8 cm) by 1" (2.7 cm) externally, and ⅜"+ (1 cm) wide. The minimum width of the handle is 1" (2.6 cm), by ¾" (1.9 cm) deep.

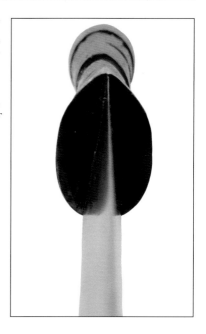

Figs. 82 and 83, *above*: View below handle, with blade edge to the left, and showing the flange of the lower ferrule overlapping the handle

Right: View below handle, with blade edge uppermost. *Courtesy of David Oliver*

The blade is plain, without any of the light beveling seen on the thick backs of the Tonybaun and Ballycolliton skeans. Here the broad back of the blade is flat and unadorned except for the incised date, 1677.

The pommel end of the skean is notable, with iron wedges driven into the wood to tighten the fit of the ferrules. In this case the wedges are hammered in according to a zigzag pattern, exactly like that seen on the pommel end of the Corbally long skean (see pages 67 and 68).

Figs. 84 and 85. Edinburgh skean laid flat, with blade edge to the left, and, *right*, the same, with the blade edge to the right. *Courtesy of David Oliver*

Figs. 86 and 87, *above*: Pommel end of handle, showing overlap of ferrule flange around the rim, with inlaid iron wedges sunk into the wood in a zigzag ornamental pattern. The pattern is rough but has the effect of "ΛΙΛΙΛΙΛ." The same treatment of the pommel end is also found on the Corbally skean (see page 68, *below*).

Below: The same, with a perspective of the handle with the blade edge turned downward. *Courtesy of David Oliver*

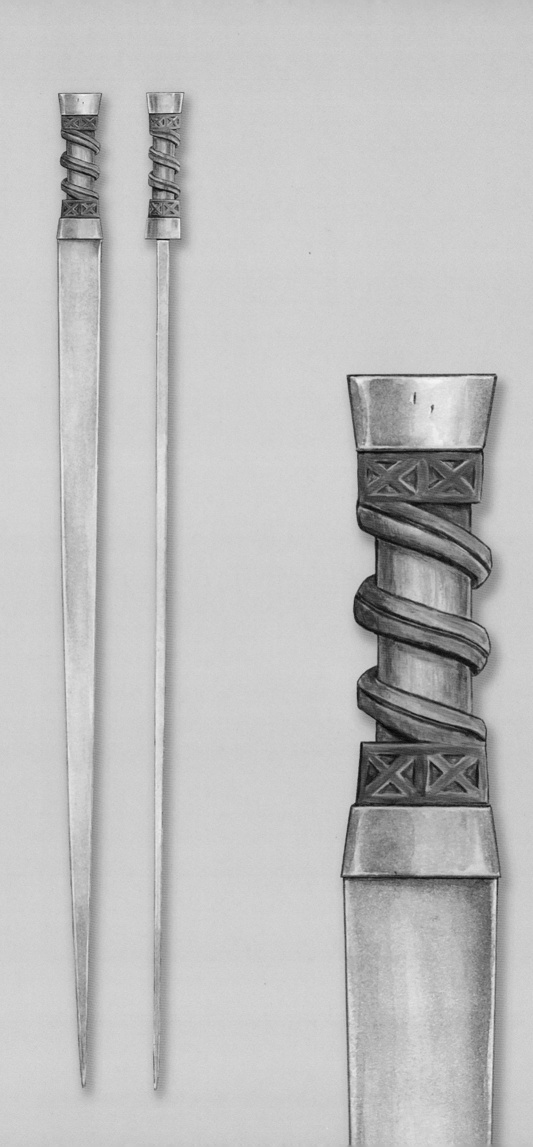

CORBALLY SKEAN

Limerick Museum reg. no. C16-17, found in river Shannon at Corbally Townland, County Limerick.

Discovered point down in the riverbed by diver Frank Hogan in 1979, this *scian fada* was recognized as an Irish skean only after the 1981 discovery of a skean with a similar handle from the river Corrib, in Dangan Lower, 2 miles upriver from Galway city.[2]

Overall length is 26" (66.5 cm), blade length is 22" (56.2 cm), width at shoulders is 2" (5.2 cm), and thickness of blade back at shoulders is ½" (1.2 cm). There are traces of a bronze scabbard fitting (ferrule) on the blade, 1⅛" (2.8 cm) below handle. The last 2⅞" (7.4 cm) of the blade was corrosion-free due to the presence of the remains of a chape of bronze wire, since lost.

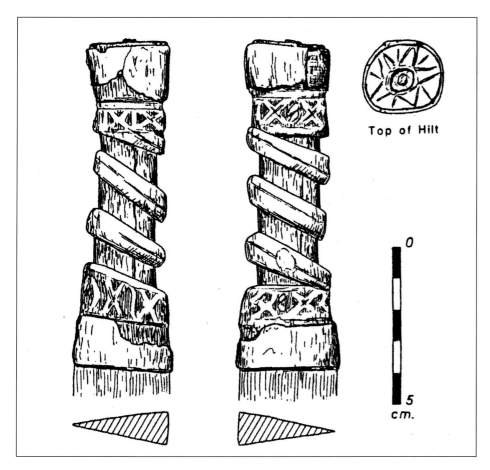

Scheme of Carving

Fig. 89. Rynne's drawings of the Corbally skean handle. *Courtesy of the Thomond Archaeological Society*

Fig. 88. Photo of Corbally skean, with blade edge to right. *Courtesy of Limerick Museum*

Fig. 91. Pommel top of the Corbally skean, with countersunk iron collar/nut to take the tang, and showing overlap of ferrule flange around the rim, with inlaid iron wedges sunk into the wood in a zigzag ornamental pattern. *Courtesy of Limerick Museum*

Fig. 90. Two sides of the Corbally skean handle, both showing the thick back of the blade, marked in white with the museum number. Note the lower ferrule is flatter than the upper ferrule. *Courtesy of Limerick Museum*

The wooden handle is 4¼6"(10.3 cm) long, deeply carved with a spiraling groove ³⁄₁₆" (4 mm) deep and ⁶⁄₁₆" (8 or 9 mm) wide, producing a raised band of similar width scored with a central line. Above and below the spiral grip are bands of raised Xs alternating with vertical ridges. The handle is bound with iron ferrules at either end, ⅝" (1.6 cm) wide. The handle is 1⅛" (2.9 cm) in diameter at its top, including the ferrule. The hilt is retained by a small washer-like piece of iron affixed to the end of the tang. The wood around the washer is filled with a zigzag, arrow-like pattern of embedded iron wedges.

Rynne notes that his initial impression, on the basis of the diver's drawing (fig. 94, page 70) was that this knife was a nineteenth-century Scottish revival dirk. With the discovery of the River Corrib skean in 1981, it became apparent that this was an Irish type, and the Corbally skean was retrieved from Sotheby's auction house in London, where it was on sale as possibly Native American.

Here is the official museum description:

Dagger, iron with wooden handle. Triangular single[-]edge blade, the spine a low V cross section. The wooden handle is cylindrical, cut out along the central portion to form a three[-]loop spiral ridge in false relief, a shallow groove along the spine of the ridge. The handle is strengthened at either end with an iron hoop, formerly flush with the surface of the handle.

The areas between the hoops and the spiral section are ornamented with motifs in false relief formed by cut out [cutout] triangles and lozenges, a narrow ridge being formed to each side of the ornamented bands. The end of the handle is held in place by a sunken washer over the end of the tang, which is hammered. The wood around the washer is iron impregnated and may have had zig-zag ornament. Centre of gravity 5¹⁵⁄₁₆" (15 cm) below handle. Conserved.

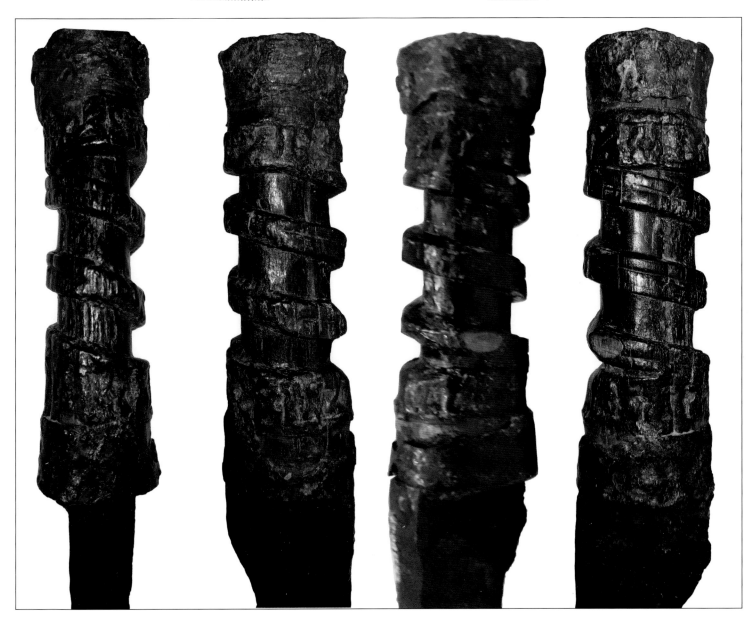

Fig. 92, *above*: Four views of the Corbally skean handle, giving full round perspective. *From left to right*: Handle with blade edge facing viewer; handle with blade edge to left; handle with thick back of blade toward viewer; handle with blade edge to right. *Courtesy of Limerick Museum*

Fig. 93, *right*: Close-up view below Corbally skean handle, with blade edge to the right; too corroded to say whether a flange on the lower ferrule overlaps the wood of the handle. *Courtesy of Limerick Museum*

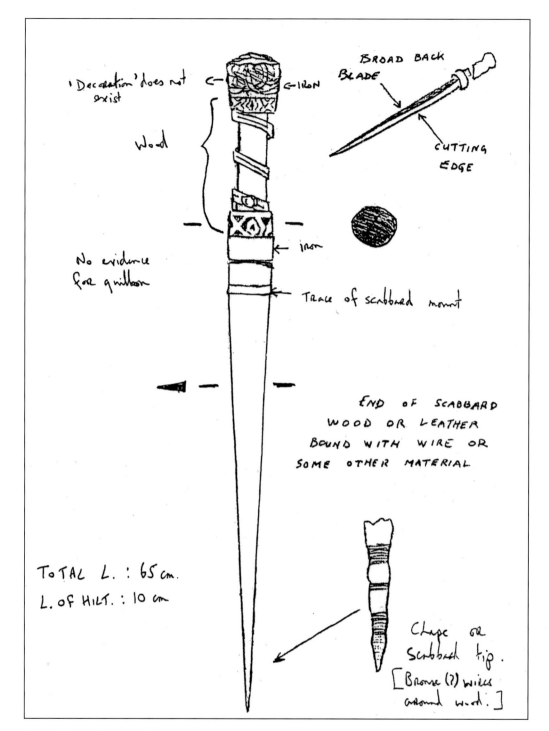

'Decoration' does not exist

← ← IRON

Wood

No evidence for guillon

BROAD BACK BLADE

CUTTING EDGE

iron

Trace of scabbard mount

END OF SCABBARD WOOD OR LEATHER BOUND WITH WIRE OR SOME OTHER MATERIAL

TOTAL L. : 65 cm.
L. OF HILT. : 10 cm

Chape or Scabbard tip. [Bronze (?) wires around wood.]

Fig. 94. Rough drawing of Corbally skean made by Frank Hogan shortly after he found it (with additional notes by National Museum staff). *Courtesy of the Thomond Archaeological Society*

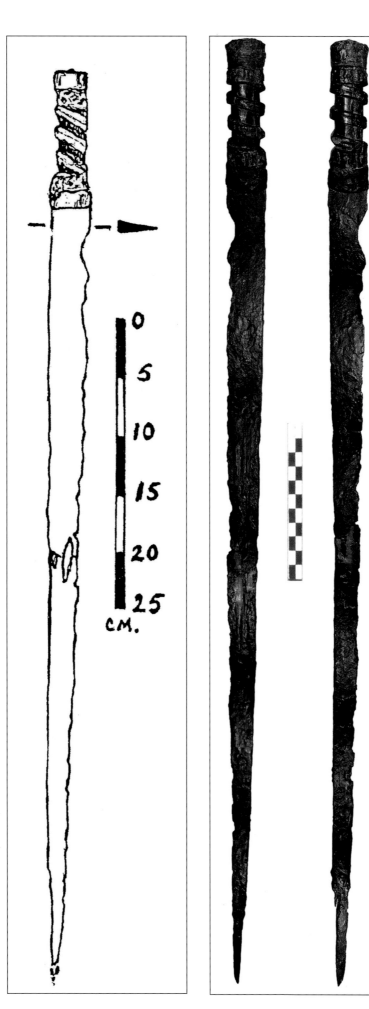

Fig. 95. Technical drawing of the Corbally skean. After Rynne. *Courtesy of the Thomond Archaeological Society*

Fig. 96. Corbally skean with blade edge to left, and, *far right*, with blade edge to right. *Courtesy of Limerick Museum*

SKEANS FROM COUNTY MEATH

One of the two long skeans on display in the National Museum as of this writing (August 2019) comes from Lagore *crannóg*, County Meath. Led by Hugh O'Neill Hencken, the Harvard Archeological Mission to Ireland arrived in 1932 and excavated Lagore *crannóg*, seeking evidence from its period as a royal residence during the Viking era. The drawings at right are from their excavation report, showing two blades identified as "scians" and labeled "E" (58 cm long) and "F" (41 cm long). These were not uncovered during the excavation, and in the report they are termed "old finds" from the site.

The National Museum has them on display but identifies them thus:

   1. Iron single-edged dagger [the longer skean, called "E" by Hencken]
   15th/16th century, Lagore crannog, Co. Meath

   2. Iron single-edged dagger [the shorter skean, called "F" by Hencken]
   15th/16th century, River Boyne, Moyfin, Co. Meath

The images at far right opposite show the thick backs of the two skean blades. Hencken says "E" is 22¾" (58 cm) long. Its tang is about 3½" (8.9 cm) long, for an actual overall length of about 26¼" (66.8 cm). It is about 1¼" (3.17 cm) wide at the shoulder, and the back of the blade is a little over ⅜" (.9 cm) thick.

Hencken's measurement for "F" is 16⁵⁄₁₆" (41 cm). It is actually about 18" (46 cm) long in the blade, with a tang a little over 4" (10 cm). It is a full 1¾" (4.4 cm) wide at the shoulders, and the back of the blade is a little over ¼" (.635 cm) thick.

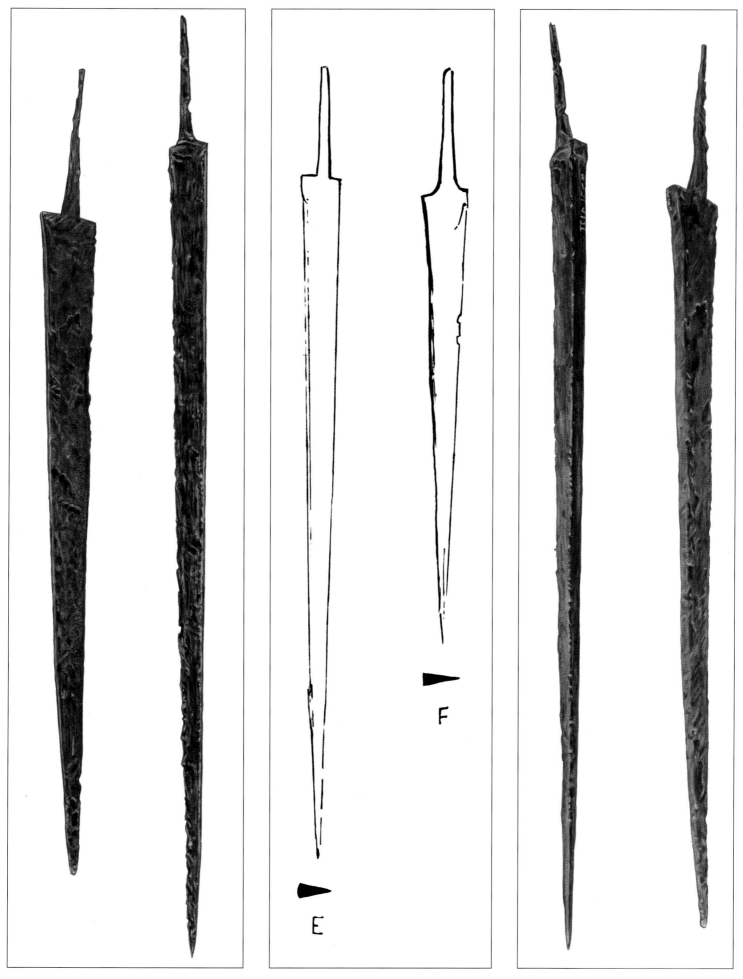

Figs. 97, 98, and 99, *above*: Long skean blades in National Museum. *Above right*: After a drawing of same from Hencken's report. *Above, far right*: The same blades, showing their thick backs.

SKEANS FROM COUNTY CARLOW

A pair of skeans were dug up together at Browne's Hill, County Carlow, in 1894. Presented that year by P. D. Vigors at a meeting of the Royal Society of Antiquaries of Ireland, but current whereabouts unknown.[3] Both were very corroded, and their handles had disappeared.

The first skean of this pair (fig. 100, *at right*) had an overall length of 18½" (46.9 cm), with a small part of the point, probably about 2" (5 cm), missing. The length of the tang was 5½" (13.2 cm), and the breadth of the blade at the hilt was 2¼" (5.7 cm), probably originally 2⁹⁄₁₆" (6.5 cm). The thickness of the blade was ¼" (0.635 cm). We are told that both "the back and edge are straight," emphasizing that it was single edged. There was an iron ring for the handle found with this skean, but it was so corroded that it fell to pieces.

Vigors recognized that this example "in no way differs from the *scian*, or knife, very commonly found in some of our oldest crannogs," and he likened it to the "dirks worn by officers in the Highland regiments." Rynne tentatively assigned this skean to his series of skeans, basing his judgment on these published descriptions and drawings. He says, "Although appreciably larger, it closely approaches the Ballycolliton weapon in its general proportions, having a blade relatively short in proportion to its width, which was originally about 14³⁰⁄₃₂" (38 cm) long and 2⁹⁄₁₆" (6.5 cm) wide at the shoulders. Furthermore, when found it had an 'iron ring for the handle' which was, unfortunately, 'so corroded it fell to pieces.'"

The second of these (fig. 101, *at far right*) is closest to the "dadagh" of O'Donovan, having a damaged cross guard of remarkably similar form still in place. Its total length, including tang, was 21" (53.3 cm). The tang was 5¾" (14.6 cm), the breadth of the blade at the hilt was 1¾" (4.4 cm), tapering to the point; a small part of the blade was missing at the point. The thickness of the blade at the hilt was ¼" (0.635 cm). The length of the cross guard was

3½" (8.9 cm). An iron ring for the handle was still in place around the tang and measured 1" (2.54 cm) in interior diameter, being ⅝" (1.6 cm) broad. Might the ring's narrow diameter suggest that the handle may have been of antler rather than wood?

G. J. Hewson, a society fellow, subsequently argued convincingly that these two skeans were likely later than Vigors's suggested twelfth-century date, citing evidence from the depositions on the Irish uprising of 1641 to place

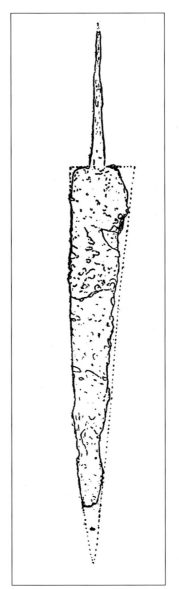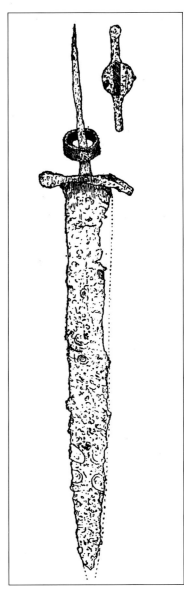

Fig. 100. First skean from Browne's Hill, County Carlow. *PD-US-expired*

Fig. 101. Second skean from Browne's Hill, County Carlow. One-half of the cross guard is forcibly bent. Vigors suggests the guard was of bronze. This and the long tang and narrow ferrule make a close comparison with the "dadagh" of O'Donovan (page 34, *above*). *PD-US-expired*

them in a sixteenth/seventeenth-century context. Hewson also made the connection between the second skean and the "dadagh" of the O'Donovan (ca. 1559), which also has a "cross-guard, which seems to be very rare in such weapons."

Vigors himself made a comparison of the second skean, with a cross guard, to a drawing by DuNoyer of a "skean dubh," now in the National Library of Ireland, which was, however, obviously a ballock knife, though with a thick back and single edge.

POSSIBLE SKEANS FROM THE RIVER CORRIB

Three long, single-edged knife blades were found in the river Corrib near Townparks, Galway city. Called "baselard knives" by Rynne, they all are missing any handles or ferrules.[4] Rynne seemed to think they were civilian, comparable to some from England identified by Ward-Perkins as baselard knives. He did note that the Gaelic Irish Kilcumber sheath, which he thought to be early sixteenth century, seemed to be made for such a blade. While he seemed reluctant to classify these weapons as Irish skeans, he did compare the Corbally *scian fada* to them when he published it in 1986.

The longest (*far right, opposite*) was found in 1981 and has an overall length of 26" (66.1 cm), the blade being 25⁵⁄₁₆" (64.5 cm) long. It is 1¹⁄₁₆" (2.7 cm) wide at the shoulders.

The other two are of nearly equal length and were found in 1982. That with a bent blade (*middle, opposite*) is 19¹³⁄₁₆" (50.3 cm) at present. Straightened out, it would be 25⁵⁄₁₆" (64.3 cm).

The last (*left, opposite*), without a tang, is 22¼" (56.5 cm) long at present.

Without a diagnostic handle in place, it is hard to identify these blades. They are a bit long and slender when compared to the long skeans reviewed above, but it was thought right to include them since Etienne Rynne himself seemed to be in some doubt whether to classify them as civilian "baselard knives" of English type, or Irish long skeans.

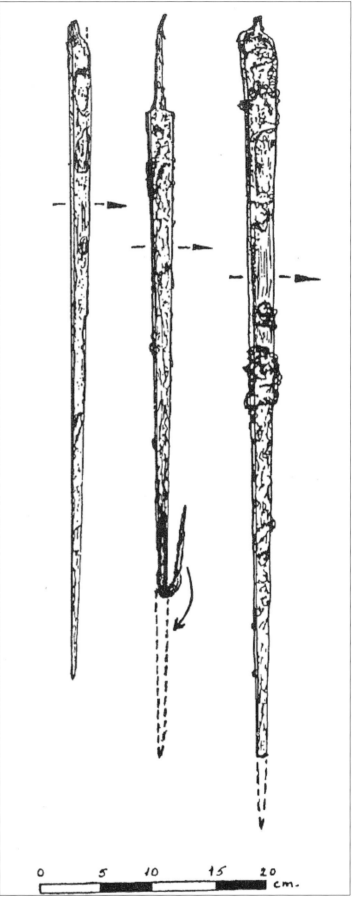

Fig. 102. Three long, slender "baselard knife" blades from the river Corrib near Townparks, Galway city. After Rynne. *Courtesy of the Galway Archaeological and Historical Society*

APPENDIX:
BARDIC POEM ON A SKEAN

A PRECIOUS WEAPON, TADHG DALL Ó HUIGINN, †1591

Welcome art thou, fierce *Gráinne*! No ill case his who should depend on thee as his only weapon, thou shining one with the hue of ruddy drops (?), well-omened, keen-edged, perilous.

Thou surpassing jewel of a *sgine*; thou venomous, inimical monster; thou form so harsh yet most smooth, dark and graceful; thou veritable queen amongst the weapons of Ireland.

Thou fierce, hacking bear; thou best of all iron; thou bright-looped, swarthy tribal treasure; thou disturber of the hearts of champions.

Thou point that cannot be withstood; thou darling of high-kings; thou black opening of the great door, thou light of even before dark.

Thou slitting of the thread of life; thou high-king amongst weapons of all kinds; thou cause of envy in the heart; treasure of the eye of multitudes.

Thou gracefully shaped bar of steel; never did thy opponent in battle bear tidings from the conflict in which ye met, nor shall one ever do so.

Even the testament (?) in short, though the fee for leeching be small—great reproach doth it bring to thy bright form—is not procured for thy victims (?).

Never did any on earth experience a bad year from thy fortune, thou brightly-blossomed, comely sun.

It was a happy omen whereby thou didst fall to *Aodh Óg*, son of this *Aodh*, to a royal heir of Conn's race; a meet comrade for thee.

Thou art such a precious treasure as sufficeth him, thou seasoned, keen, cool weapon, and he, the youth from Bregia's battlesome castle, is the one sufficing surety for thee.

Oft, as a pledge of much wealth, hast thou been lifted from the smooth, comely knee of Maeve's descendant, at the quaffing of the juice of the vine-fruit.

Oft, it is said, as stipend of a high-king's heir, did the salmon from the fertile, murmuring Boyne get much gold and silver by thy means.

Oft hath a hundred of each kind of cattle been readily got through thee by *Aodh* for the poets of *Crioinhthann's* line, to uphold the repute of the stately, heavy-lashed one

Never was it expected, thou shining one that hast not suffered hurt, that the scion from ancient *Aolmhagh's* slender streams would forego thee for the excellent weapons of any of the men of Ireland.

None of the men of the world could obtain thee from the white-toothed, graceful one—bright palm to which one must needs yield homage—save some man of art.

In exchange for gold or silver none might get thee readily from the prop of Bregia's white-footed host; and it is not likely that thou wouldst be obtained by force.

From the chieftain of *Eachaidh's*, race an exacting poet accepted nothing on earth save thee alone; thus was it easier to obtain thee.

Since one hath sought thee, after this *Aodh*, thou noble, alert, smooth, studded weapon, nobody will be forbearing towards any poet.

ENDNOTES

Preface

1. Patrick J. Duffy, David Edwards, and Elizabeth Fitzpatrick, eds., *Gaelic Ireland, Land, Lordship & Settlement, ca. 1250–ca.1650* (Bodmin, UK: Four Courts, 2001), 67.

2. Gerard A. Hayes-McCoy, *Sixteenth Century Irish Swords* (Dublin: National Museum of Ireland, 1959), 18.

Chapter 1: History of the Skean

1. Charles Smith, *Ancient and Present State of the County and City of Cork*, vol. 2 (Dublin, 1749), 414.

2. Katharine Simms, *From Kings to Warlords* (Woodbridge, UK: Boydell, 1987), 17.

3. Tobias Capwell, *The World Encyclopedia of Knives, Daggers and Bayonets* (London: Hermes House, 2009), 30–31.

4. "The People of the Blade," *Old European Culture* blog, March 17, 2014, https://oldeuropeanculture. blogspot.com.

5. Charles E. Whitelaw, "The Origin and Development of the Highland Dirk," *Transactions of the Glasgow Archaeological Society* 5 (1905): 32–42.

6. James D. Forman, *The Scottish Dirk* (Alexandria Bay, NY, and Bloomfield, ON: Museum Restoration Service, 1991), 8.

7. Ibid., 6.

8. John Wallace, *Scottish Swords and Dirks: An Illustrated Reference Guide to Scottish Edged Weapons* (Mechanicsburg, PA: Stackpole Books, 1970), 57.

9. K. A. Steer and J. W. M. Bannerman, *Late Medieval Monumental Sculpture in the West Highlands* (Norwich, UK: Her Majesty's Stationery Office, 1977), 172.

10. Francis Collinson, *The Traditional and National Music of Scotland* (London: Routledge and Kegan Paul, 1966), 97.

11. N. J. A. Williams, ed., *Pairlement Chloinne Tomáis* (Dublin: Dublin Institute for Advanced Studies, 1981), 167.

12. Capwell, *The World Encyclopedia of Knives, Daggers and Bayonets*, 51.

13. William Forbes Skene, *Memorials of the Family of Skene of Skene, from the Family Papers, with Other Illustrative Documents* (Aberdeen, Scotland: New Spaulding Club, 1887), 6.

14. Sir George Mackenzie, *Science of Heraldry*, 1680, 5.

15. Skene, *Memorials of the Family of Skene of Skene, from the Family Papers, with Other Illustrative Documents*, 8.

16. Lambert MacKenna, ed., *The Book of Magauran* (Dublin, Ireland: Dublin Institute for Advanced Studies, 1947), 290, 323.

17. Peter Harbison, "Native Irish Arms and Armour in Medieval Gaelic Literature, 1170–1600," *Irish Sword: Journal of the Military History Society of Ireland* 12, no. 48 (1976): 174.

18. Richard Hayes, "Irish Soldiers at the Siege of Rouen (1418–19)," *Irish Sword: Journal of the Military History Society of Ireland* 2, no. 5 (1954): 63.

19. Ibid., 62.

20. Steve Muhlberger, ed., *Tales of Froissart*, Book IV, chap. 64 (Johnes, 2:577–82), Nipissing University, https://uts.nipissingu.ca/muhlberger/FROISSART/IRELAND.HTM.

21. L. Price, ed., "Armed Forces of the Irish Chiefs in the Early Sixteenth Century," *Journal of the Royal Society of Antiquaries of Ireland* 62 (1932): 206.

22. Raphael Holinshed, *Chronicles of England, Scotlande and Irelande*, vol. 6 (Abingdon, UK: Routledge, 1965), 132, http://books.google.com.

23. Hans Hamilton, ed., *Calendar of the State Papers Relating to Ireland (CSPI)*, vol. 4 (London: HMSO, 1885), 54.

24. Ibid., vol. 6 (London: HMSO, 1890), 322.

25. Litton Falkiner, *Illustrations of Irish History and Topography* (London: Longmans, Green, 1904), 357.

26. Hans Hamilton, ed., *CSPI*, vol. 2 (London: Longmans, Green, Reader & Dyer, 1867), 365.

27. Hans Hamilton, ed., *CSPI*, vol. 4 (London: HMSO, 1885), 264.

28. Joseph Walker, *An Historical Essay on the Dress of the Ancient and Modern Irish* (Dublin, Ireland: George Grierson, 1788), 87.

29. Mary Hickson, *Ireland in the Seventeenth Century, &c.*, vol. II (London: Longmans, Green, 1884), 67.

30. Henry Morris, "Meadóg," *Béaloideas, a Journal of Irish Folklore* 9 (1931): 291.

31. Laurent Vital, *Le Premier Voyage de Charles-Quint en Espagne, de 1517 à 1518*, https://celt.ucc.ie//published/T500000-001/.

32. Hans Hamilton, ed., *CSPI*, vol. 1 (London: Green, Longman & Roberts, 1860), 86.

33. John Derricke, *The Image of Ireland; With a Discourie of Woodkarne*, 1581 (Delmar, NY: Scholar's Facsimiles and Reprints, 1998), 54.

34. Constantia Maxwell, *Irish History from Contemporary Sources (1509–1610)* (London: George, Allen & Unwin, 1923), 320.

35. Edmund Curtis, ed., *The Calendar of Ormond Deeds, Vol. V*, Irish Manuscripts Commission (Dublin, Ireland: Stationery Office, 1932), 75.

36. Robert Steel, ed., Proclamation No. 252, April 1, 1624, *Tudor and Stuart Proclamations, 1485–1714*, vol. 2, *Scotland & Ireland* (Oxford: Clarendon, 1910), 27.

37. "Varia," *Béaloideas, a Journal of Irish Folklore* 10 (1940): 288.

38. Ibid., 289.

39. James Berry, *Tales of Mayo and Connemara* (Salem, NH: Salem House, 1984), 120.

40. Joseph Walker, *An Historical Essay on the Dress of the Ancient and Modern Irish* (Dublin, Ireland: George Grierson, 1788), 119.

41. Maxwell, *Irish History from Contemporary Sources (1509–1610)*, 221.

42. Gerard A. Hayes-McCoy, *Irish Battles* (London: Longmans, 1969), 110.

43. Thomas Stafford, *Pacata Hibernia*, vol. 1, ed. Standish O'Grady (London: Downey, 1896), 122.

44. Rev. C. P. Meehan, *The Fate and Fortunes of Tyrone and Tyrconnel*, 2nd ed. (London: James Duffy, 1870), 56.

45. Litton C. Falkiner, *Illustrations of Irish History and Topography, Mainly of the Seventeenth Century* (London: Longmans, Green, 1904), 388.

46. Roderic O'Flaherty, *A Chorographical Description of West Or H-Iar Connaught: Written A.D. 1684* (Dublin, Ireland: M. H. Gill University Press, 1846), 407.

47. Jonah Barrington, *Personal Sketches of His Own Times*, vol. 1 (London: Henry Colburn and Richard Bentley, 1830), 32.

48. Edward MacLysaght, *Irish Life in the Seventeenth Century* (Cork, Ireland: University Press, 1950), 362.

49. J. O. Bartley, *Teague, Shenkin and Sawney* (Cork, Ireland: University Press, 1954), 322.

50. James Anthony Froude, *The English in Ireland in the Eighteenth Century*, vol. 1 (London: Longmans, Green, 1872), 443.

Chapter 2: Manufacture and Possible Export of the Skean

1. Michael M. Barkham, "The Spanish Basque Irish Fishery & Trade in the Sixteenth Century," *History Ireland* 9 (2001): 12–15.

2. Hickson, *Ireland in the Seventeenth Century*, 376.

3. Paul Rondelez, "Ironworking in Late Medieval Ireland, ca. AD 1250 to 1600," vol. 1 (PhD diss., University College Cork, 2014), 35.

4. Etienne Rynne, "Three Irish Knife-Daggers," *Journal of the Royal Society of Antiquaries of Ireland* 99 (1969): 137–43.

5. Rondelez, "Ironworking in Late Medieval Ireland, ca. AD 1250 to 1600," 1:35.

6. "Blacksmiths and the Supernatural," *Ireland's Folklore and Traditions* blog, March 13, 2017, https://irishfolklore.wordpress.com.

7. Hugh Allingham, *Captain Cuellar's Adventures in Connacht and Ulster, A.D. 1588* (London: Elliot Stock, 1897), 60.

8. Rondelez, "Ironworking in Late Medieval Ireland, ca. AD 1250 to 1600," 1:202.

Chapter 3: Fighting Techniques

1. Graham Kew, ed., "Fynes Moryson's Unpublished Itinerary," *Analecta Hibernica* 37 (1998): 110.

2. William Alexander Gordon, *Recollections of a Highland Subaltern, during the Campaigns of the 93rd Highlanders in India* (London: Edward Arnold, 1898), 61.

3. Thomas Crofton Croker, *The Tour of the French Traveller, M. Boullaye LeGouz, in Ireland, A.D. 1644* (London: T. and W. Boone, 1837), 42.

4. Standish O'Grady, ed., *Thomas Stafford's Pacata Hibernia*, vol. 1 (London: Downey, 1896), 22.

5. A. MacGregor, *Lecture on the Art of Defense* (Paisley, Scotland: J. Neilson, 1791), 72.

6. Kate Chadbourne, "The Knife against the Wave," *Béaloideas, a Journal of Irish Folklore* 80 (2012): 70–85.

7. Capwell, *The World Encyclopedia of Knives, Daggers and Bayonets*, 26.

8. Archibald M'Sparran, *The Irish Legend; or M'Donnell and the Norman de Burgos,* (Coleraine: J. M'Combie, 1854), 103.

9. Hayes-McCoy, *Irish Battles,* 101.

Chapter 4: Morphology and Sheaths

1. L. F. MacNamara, ed., "The Cathreim Thoirdhealbhaigh Manuscripts and O'Grady's Edition," *Modern Philology* 59, no. 2 (1961): 122–25.

2. I. J. Buckley, "Some Early Ornamental Leatherwork," *Journal of the Royal Society of Antiquaries of Ireland* 5, no. 1 (1915): 305.

3. Etienne Rynne, "Military and Civilian Swords from the River Corrib," *Journal of the Galway Archaeological and Historical Society* 39 (1983/1984): 5–26.

Chapter 5: Short Skeans, or *Miodóga*

1. Smith, *Ancient and Present State of the County and City of Cork*, 2:414.

2. "Proceedings," *Journal of the Royal Historical and Archaeological Association of Ireland* 5, 4th series (1879–82): 443.

3. Etienne Rynne, "Three Irish Knife-Daggers," *Journal of the Royal Society of Antiquaries of Ireland* 99 (1969): 137–43.

4. Ibid..

5. Ibid.

Chapter 6: Long Skeans, or *Sciana Fada*

1. Etienne Rynne, "A 16th or 17th Century Skean from the River Shannon," *North Munster Antiquarian Journal* 28 (1986): 40–45.

2. Ibid..

3. P. D. Vigors, "Two Recently Discovered Iron Sword-Dirks from the County Carlow," *Journal of the Royal Historical and Archaeological Association of Ireland* 24 (1894): 190–92.

4. Etienne Rynne, "Military and Civilian Swords from the River Corrib," *Journal of the Galway Archaeological and Historical Society* 39 (1983/1984): 5–26.

Appendix

1. Eleanor Knott, ed., *The Bardic Poems of Tadhg Dall O'Huiginn (1550–1591)*, vol. 2 (London: Simpkin, Marshall, Hamilton, Kent, 1922), 160.

BIBLIOGRAPHY

Allingham, Hugh. *Captain Cuellar's Adventures in Connacht and Ulster, A.D. 1588*. London: Elliot Stock, 1897.

Barkham, Michael. "The Spanish Basque Irish Fishery & Trade in the Sixteenth Century." *History Ireland* 9 (2001): 12–15.

Barrington, Jonah. *Personal Sketches of His Own Times*. Vol. 1. London: Henry Colburn and Richard Bentley, 1830.

Bartley, J. O. *Teague, Shenkin and Sawney*. Cork, Ireland: University Press, 1954.

Berry, James. *Tales of Mayo and Connemara*. Salem, NH: Salem House, 1984.

Buckley, I. J. "Some Early Ornamental Leatherwork." *Journal of the Royal Society of Antiquaries of Ireland* 5, no. 1 (1915): 305.

Cameron, Esther. *Scabbards and Sheaths from Viking and Medieval Dublin*. Bilbao, Spain: Estudios Gráphicos Zure, 2007.

Capwell, Tobias. *The World Encyclopedia of Knives, Daggers and Bayonets*. London: Hermes House, 2009.

Chadbourne, Kate. "The Knife against the Wave." *Béaloideas, a Journal of Irish Folklore* 80 (2012): 70–85.

Collinson, Francis. *The Traditional and National Music of Scotland*. London: Routledge and Kegan Paul, 1966.

Croker, Thomas Crofton. *The Tour of the French Traveller, M. Boullaye LeGouz, in Ireland, A.D. 1644*. London: T. and W. Boone, 1837.

Curtis, Edmund, ed. *The Calendar of Ormond Deeds*. Dublin, Ireland: Stationery Office, 1932.

Duffy, Patrick J., David Edwards, and Elizabeth Fitzpatrick, eds. *Gaelic Ireland, Land, Lordship & Settlement, ca. 1250–ca. 1650*. Bodmin, UK: Four Courts, 2001.

Falkiner, Litton C. *Illustrations of Irish History and Topography, Mainly of the Seventeenth Century*. London: Longmans, Green, 1904.

Forman, James D. *The Scottish Dirk*. Alexandria Bay, NY, and Bloomfield, ON: Museum Restoration Service, 1991.

Froude, James Anthony. *The English in Ireland in the Eighteenth Century*. Vol. 1. London: Longmans, Green, 1872.

Gordon, William Alexander. *Recollections of a Highland Subaltern, during the Campaigns of the 93rd Highlanders in India*. London: Edward Arnold, 1898.

Hamilton, Hans, ed. *Calendar of the State Papers Relating to Ireland (CSPI)*. 24 vols. London: 1860–1912.

Harbison, Peter. "Native Irish Arms and Armour in Medieval Gaelic Literature, 1170–1600." *Irish Sword: Journal of the Military History Society of Ireland* 12, no. 48 (1976): 173–99.

Hayes, Richard. "Irish Soldiers at the Siege of Rouen (1418–19)." *Irish Sword: Journal of the Military History Society of Ireland* 2, no. 5 (1954): 63.

Hayes-McCoy, Gerard A. *Irish Battles*. London: Longmans, 1969.

Hayes-McCoy, Gerard A. *Sixteenth Century Irish Swords*. Dublin: National Museum of Ireland, 1959.

Hickson, Mary. *Ireland in the Seventeenth Century, &c.* Vol. 2. London: Longmans, Green, 1884.

Kelly, Fergus. *A Guide to Early Irish Law*. Dublin, Ireland: Institute for Advanced Studies, 1988.

Kew, Graham. ed. "Fynes Moryson's Unpublished Itinerary." *Analecta Hibernica*, No. 37 (1998): 3-137.

Knott, Eleanor, ed. *The Bardic Poems of Tadhg Dall O'Huiginn (1550–1591)*. Vol. 2. London: Simpkin, Marshall, Hamilton, Kent, 1922.

MacGregor, A. *Lecture on the Art of Defense*. Paisley, Scotland: J. Neilson, 1791.

MacKenna, Lambert, ed. *The Book of Magauran*. Dublin, Ireland: Dublin Institute for Advanced Studies, 1947.

MacLysaght, Edward. *Irish Life in the Seventeenth Century*. Cork, Ireland: University Press, 1950.

MacNamara, L. F., ed. "The Cathreim Thoirdhealbhaigh Manuscripts and O'Grady's Edition." *Modern Philology* 59, no. 2 (1961): 122–25.

Maxwell, Constantia. *Irish History from Contemporary Sources (1509–1610)*. London: George, Allen & Unwin, 1923.

Meehan, Rev. C. P. *The Fate and Fortunes of Tyrone and Tyrconnel*. 2nd ed. London: James Duffy, 1870.

Morris, Henry. "Meadóg," *Béaloideas, a Journal of Irish Folklore* 9 (1931): 291.

M'Sparran, Archibald. *The Irish Legend; or M'Donnell and the Norman de Burgos*. Coleraine: J. M'Combie, 1854.

O'Grady, Standish, ed. *Thomas Stafford's Pacata Hibernia*. London: Downey, 1896.

Price, L. "Armed Forces of the Irish Chiefs in the Early Sixteenth Century." *Journal of the Royal Society of Antiquaries of Ireland* 62 (1932): 206.

Rondelez, Paul. "Ironworking in Late Medieval Ireland, ca. AD 1250 to 1600." PhD diss., University College Cork, 2014.

Rynne, Etienne. "Military and Civilian Swords from the River Corrib." *Journal of the Galway Archaeological and Historical Society* 39 (1984): 5–26.

———. "A 16th or 17th Century Skean from the River Shannon." *North Munster Antiquarian Journal* 28 (1986): 40–45.

———. "Three Irish Knife-Daggers." *Journal of the Royal Society of Antiquaries of Ireland* 99 (1969): 137–43.

Simms, Katherine. *From Kings to Warlords*. Woodbridge, UK: Boydell, 1987.

Skene, William Forbes. *Memorials of the Family of Skene of Skene, from the Family Papers, with Other Illustrative Documents*. Aberdeen, Scotland: New Spaulding Club, 1887.

Smith, Charles. *Ancient and Present State of the County and City of Cork*. Dublin, 1749.

Steer, K. A., and J. W. M. Bannerman. *Late Medieval Monumental Sculpture in the West Highlands*. Norwich, UK: Her Majesty's Stationery Office, 1977.

Vigors, P. D. "Two Recently Discovered Iron Sword-Dirks from the County Carlow." *Journal of the Royal Historical and Archaeological Association of Ireland* 24 (1894): 190–92.

Walker, Joseph. *An Historical Essay on the Dress of the Ancient and Modern Irish*. Dublin, Ireland: George Grierson, 1788.

Wallace, John. *Scottish Swords and Dirks: An Illustrated Reference Guide to Scottish Edged Weapons*. Mechanicsburg, PA: Stackpole Books, 1970.

Whitelaw, Charles E. "The Origin and Development of the Highland Dirk." *Transactions of the Glasgow Archaeological Society* 5 (1905): 32–42.

Williams, N. J. A., ed. *Pairlement Chloinne Tomáis*. Dublin, Ireland: Dublin Institute for Advanced Studies, 1981.

GLOSSARY

auricular: A decoration style resembling the ear, characteristic of the northern baroque

ballock: Sometimes called kidney dagger, a popular form of dagger throughout the fifteenth and sixteenth centuries

baselard: A dagger, often with an I-shaped handle, characteristic of the fourteenth and fifteenth centuries

bawn: The outer wall of an Irish castle, enclosing a courtyard into which cattle were often driven at night for safekeeping

biodag: In Scots Gaelic, a dirk

bonnaught: From Irish *bunnacht*, a hired soldier, and in the Tudor era specifically soldiers armed and trained as modern pike and shot by the rebel Irish lords

broages: From Irish *bróg*, meaning the traditional Irish shoe, single soled and sewn with leather thong

churl: Archaic term for peasant

cóta mór: In Irish, a great coat or overcoat

crannóg: A defensive lake dwelling built on an artificial island

dag: A pistol

dart: A short throwing spear, with or without flights, and characteristic of the Irish kern

dirk: Single-edged Scottish Highland dagger, similar to an Irish skean

dudgeon: A dagger characteristic of late-sixteenth/early-seventeenth-century northern England and Lowland Scotland, evolving from the ballock dagger and being a possible precursor to the dirk

dunewassell: From Scots Gaelic *duine uasal*, meaning a noble

galloglass: Heavily armed Irish foot soldier of the medieval and Tudor eras

gillieweetfoot: From Scots Gaelic *gillie-casfliuch*, the wet-footed servant who carried his master across streams

gossoon: From Irish *garsún*, a boy or lad in Irish English, via Anglo-French, Old French *garçon*

headpiece: Archaic term for helmet

horsemen's staves: Light cavalry lances, about 8 or 9 feet long.

kern: Light-armed Irish foot soldier of the medieval and Tudor eras

mantles: The traditional Irish cloaks

miodóg: In Irish, a dagger

Palesman: Inhabitant of the English Pale of settlement surrounding Dublin

peeces: Firearms in Tudor English

poignard: A long, lightweight thrusting knife with a continuously tapering, acutely pointed blade

rapparee: Irish guerrilla fighters on the Jacobite side in the 1690s Williamite war in Ireland, and subsequently bandits

rondel: A sharply pointed dagger often with disk-shaped handguard and pommel, popular from the fourteenth to sixteenth centuries

rullion: A rough shoe made of rawhide

scian: In Irish, a knife, but historically often designating a fighting knife and spelled "skean" in English

scian fada: In Irish, a long knife, specifically a long-bladed version of the skean

scull: A simple form of helmet

seanachus: Irish folklore

seax: A single-edged knife of variable size, often with a clipped point, characteristic of Germanic peoples of the Migration era and early Middle Ages

shot: Soldiers armed with firearms in the Tudor era

skean: Generally accepted English spelling of the Irish term *scian*, a knife

targe: *See* target

target: A round shield used in conjunction with a sword in the Tudor and Stuart eras

tuagh: In Irish, a battle ax, generally with a 6-foot haft, characteristic of the galloglass

terminus ante quem: The latest possible date for something

trowses: From Irish *truis*, meaning the traditional Irish trousers, fitted to the leg and looser in the body

tuyere: A nozzle through which an air blast is delivered to a forge or blast furnace

ward: The garrison of a castle

INDEX

ABOUT THE AUTHOR

Robert Gresh is a lifelong student of Irish arms and armor. He has reviewed reserve collections in Ireland and correctly identified a skean in the possession of a prominent British collector, which was mislabeled as a Scottish dirk. He is the author of several other works on the military aspects of 16th century Ireland.